BOUDIN

Sky and Sea

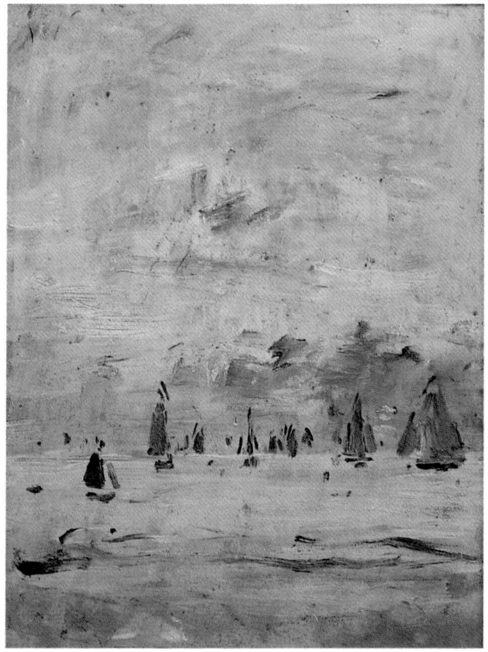

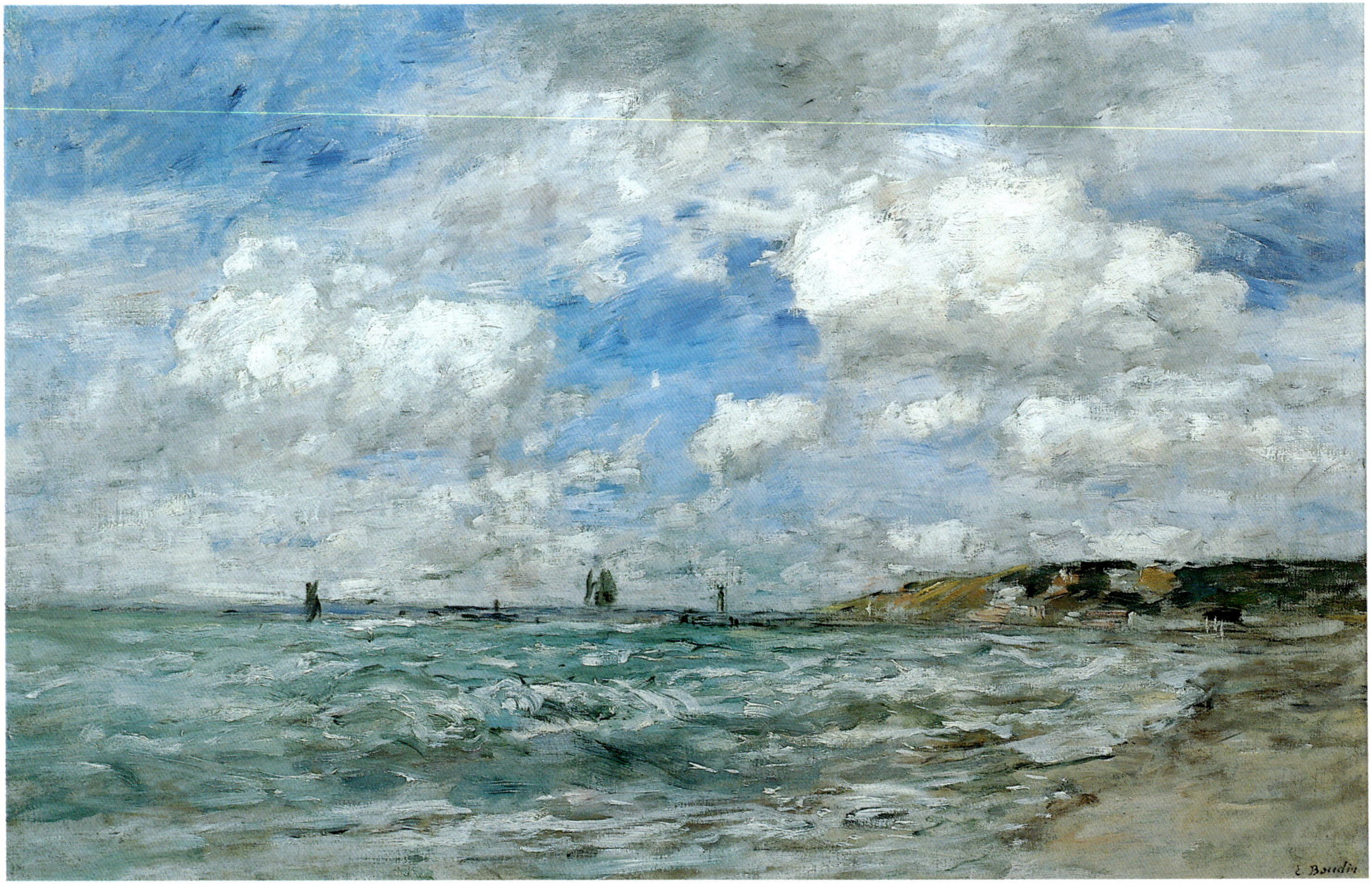

Trouville coastline, 1894-1897.

BOUDIN
Sky and Sea

Laurent Manœuvre

Translated from the french by Graham Bushnell

HERSCHER

For Anne-Marie Kuenegel

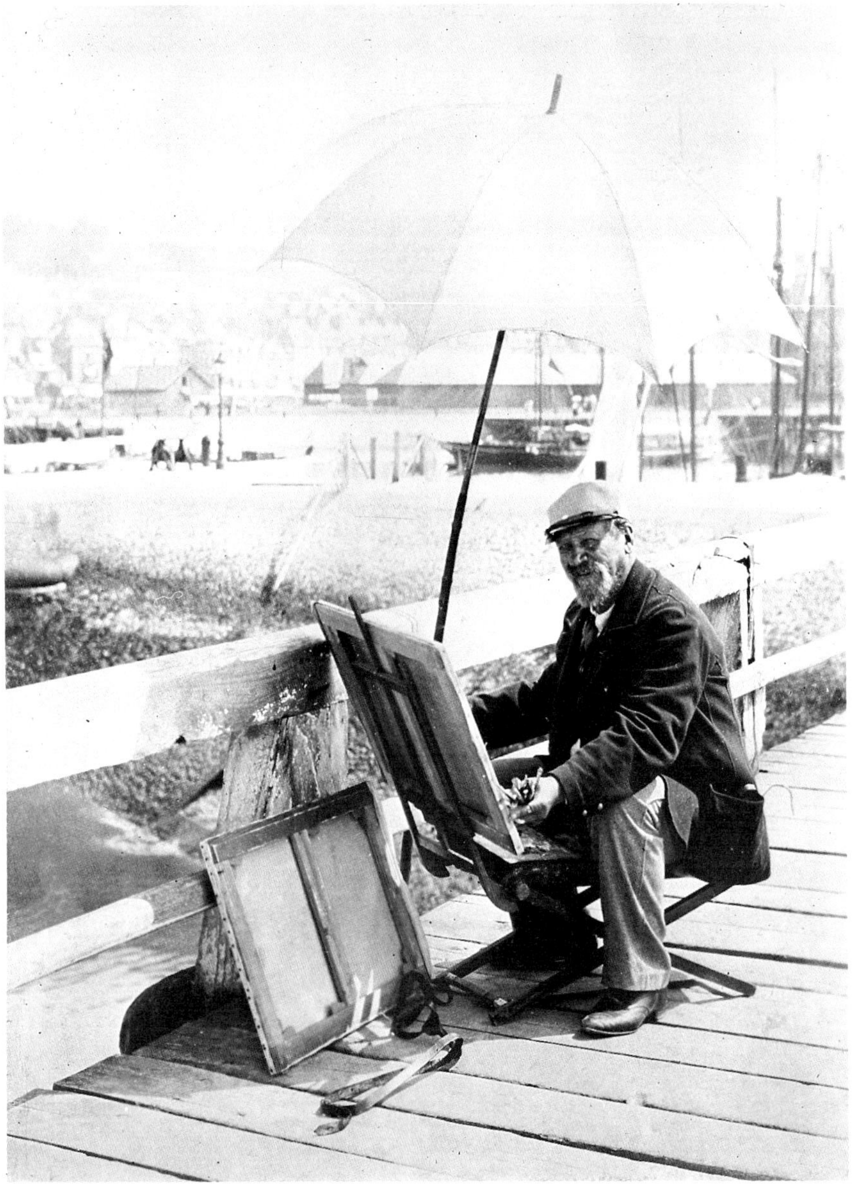

Eugène Boudin painting on the jetty at Trouville in 1896.

INTRODUCTION

Eugène Boudin is often considered to be one of the links between the School of Barbizon and Impressionism. Indeed, the year of his birth – 1824 – places him almost halfway between the two movements, though slightly nearer to the former than to the latter: eight years separate him from Théodore Rousseau, sixteen from Monet.

However, Boudin's date of birth cannot really be considered to be a true point of reference. Not only did he come to painting quite late in life, but he also chose a rather slow way of learning his new trade. Rather than frequent a particular studio, he preferred to pick things up here and there with masters like Corot, and above all to paint from nature. This rather nonconformist approach enabled him to develop his own style in complete independence. This was a long process lasting about fourteen years and during this time he was prey to doubts and hesitations. «So ends a discouraging year,» he wrote in his diary on 31st December 1854. Five years later, his friend Courbet managed to rid him of his uncertainties and, from that moment on, despite financial problems and adverse criticism, Boudin was easier in his mind and able to affirm his originality.

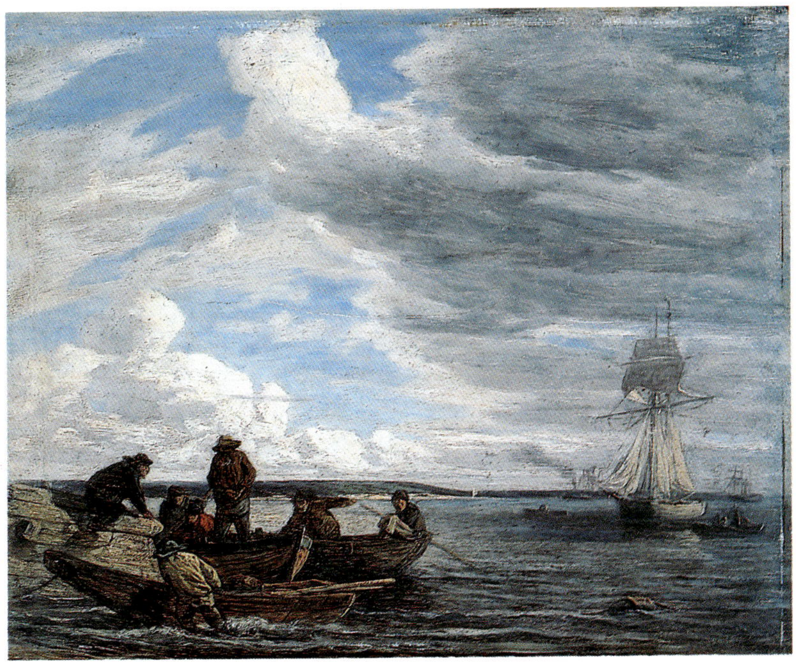

FISHERMEN OFF LE HAVRE, 1852.

His first truly innovatory paintings – the beach scenes (p. 15, p. 17) – date from 1863, the year of the scandal that surrounded Manet's *Déjeuner sur l'herbe*. From that moment, Boudin's career developed alongside that of the Impressionists, although he did not always identify himself with them. He joined the Impressionist group on the occasion of their first exhibition, but, with this one exception, he never really mixed with them. However, he was always interested in the way in which they were developing, sometimes going so far as to borrow elements from them, but never to the detriment of his own specific style. Right up to the end of his career, he continued to paint in his own manner, indifferent to the internal strife which shook the foundations of the Impressionist movement and finally broke it up: once Manet had gone, Monet edged little by little towards a dream world, Pissarro developed a passion for Neo-impressionism and Degas, who was gradually losing his sight, intensified the colour of his pastels in the strangest of ways. If it is true that, as Michel Butor remarks, «being faithful to nature is the essence of Impressionistic strategy,» Boudin alone remained a true Impressionist to the end, at least in the works offered to the public eye.

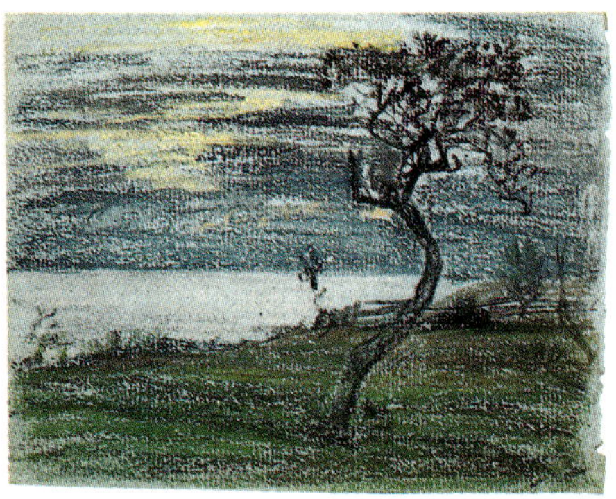

SEINE ESTUARY NEAR HONFLEUR, 1854-1860.

Boudin was born in Honfleur and was the son of a sailor. This partly explains his familiarity with the world of the sea. According to the *Guide pittoresque du voyageur en France,* a travel guide published in 1838, Honfleur's prosperity depended mainly on the port. All sorts of ships, from whalers to trawlers, were still fitted out there, and maritime trade, notably the export of agricultural produce from the surrounding countryside to England and the nordic countries was sizeable enough to warrant the presence of several vice-consulates in the town as well as a warehouse for colonial goods.

Various trades had sprung up to service the port: barrel-makers, manufacturers of sea biscuit, meat and fish salters, tanners, ropemakers and shipbuilders. But at that time, Honfleur was in keen competition with the rapidly-expanding port of Le Havre. In 1835, the attractions of the rival port caused the Boudin family to cross the estuary and settle there. However, family ties with Honfleur were never broken. Boudin's parents soon started work on the steamer which made the daily hour-and-a-quarter trip between the two towns: his father was a crew-member and his mother a maid. As for the future painter himself, he too spent his time between Honfleur and Le Havre.

The world in which Boudin grew up was to have a deep and lasting influence on him. His house in Le Havre stood on the Grand-Quai which ran alongside the port. At that time, Le Havre ranked only behind Marseilles in terms of the number of ships it handled. It was a town open to the world, full of energy and enterprise. And it was with a local enterprise – a printer's – that Boudin got his first job when he left school. He then set himself up as a stationer and picture framer, drawing in his spare time and gleaning advice from those painters who were his customers: Millet, Couture and Troyon.

He greatly admired Millet and the Barbizon painters and yet, despite this and the fact that he lived so close to the countryside, Boudin felt none of their closeness to the earth. There was however one period in the 1860s when, through his wife, he discovered the country people of Finistère. He was attracted by the austerity of their life

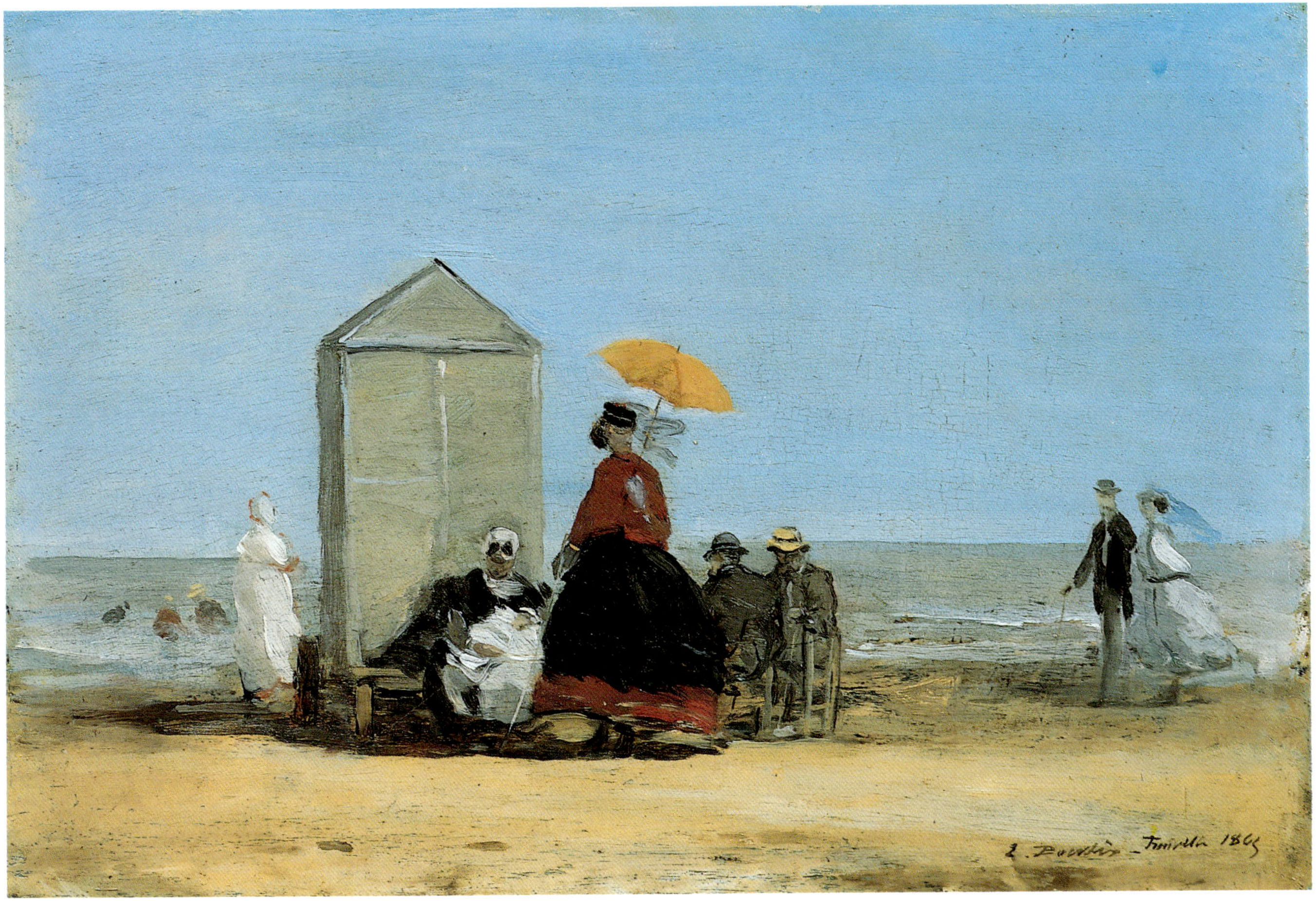

On the beach at Trouville, 1863.

and briefly turned away from his usual subjects. «Trouville beach, which I used to think so delightful, now seems on my return just a ghastly mascarade.» However, his paintings of peasant life were hardly innovatory, neither in the subject matter he chose – interiors of farms or dark churches – nor in the neo-Rembrandtesque treatment of light, which was fairly typical of the period. But this was only a passing phase, and the painter soon came

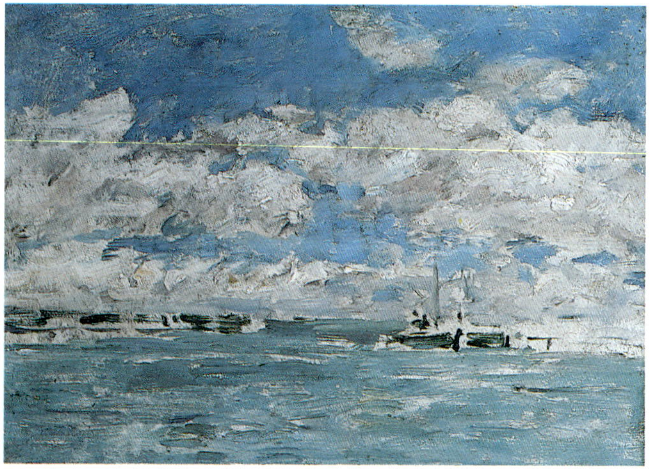

Clouds, blue sky and boats, 1895-1897.

back to the sea and the open air. Over the years, Boudin explored coastlines, from Rotterdam to Bordeaux, and from Villefranche to Venice. He would have been quite content to limit himself to his native Normandy where he found no lack of themes for inspiration, but he had to satisfy the demands of clients who wanted new seascape subjects. He was therefore obliged to look farther afield, remaining within sight of the sea or of a port even if he went inland. His choices occasionally corresponded to a specific demand (Bordeaux) or to the fashion of the moment (Berck). Although he produced successful works in these cases, his true inspiration came from vast expanses of empty beaches. «I don't like quaysides very much with their hustle-bustle of carriages, crates and barrels like Le Havre or Antwerp; a pleasant enough swirl of activity for those whose profits depend on the number of crates and barrels let down by the cranes, but there is no pleasure here for the dreamer who prefers silence and solitude, nor for the more monotonous yet more poetic voices of the elements. These commercial towns annoy me with their dust, their dirty leather, and above all the guano. These are all excellent things in their own right but one just cannot forget the healthy odour of seaweed and the irreplaceable fresh, damp, saltiness of our shores.»

Before Boudin, other talented painters had come to Honfleur, Sainte-Adresse and the surrounding area. This was at the time when the Romantics were taking a look at the picturesque aspects of traditional life in France. Always on the lookout for curiosities, artists and writers were often content to take a superficial look at these

Dusk over the Bassin du Commerce, 1892-1894.

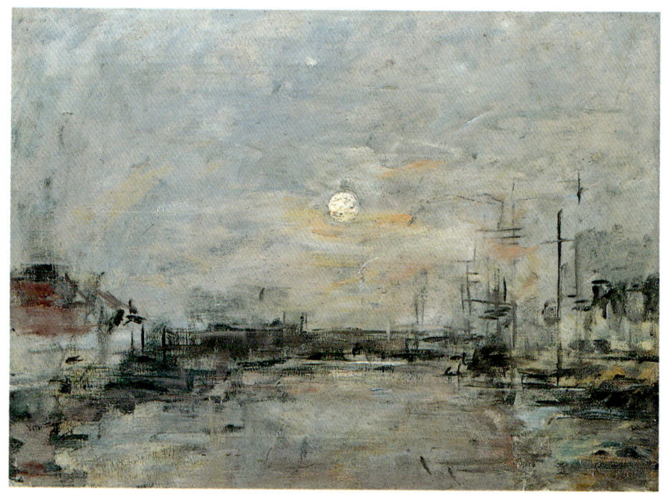

regions. Boudin proceeded differently, rather in the manner of one of his contemporaries, another native of Normandy, Gustave Flaubert. Both immersed themselves in a microcosm and extracted the essence. Flaubert, in examining the workings of human emotions, compared his approach to that of a doctor doing an autopsy, scalpel in hand. In the same way, Boudin ignored the conventional aspects of Normandy so dear to the hearts of tourists – thatched roofs, apple trees, cliffs and traditional costumes – and attached himself to the meticulously faithful description of a place in its finest detail, seen at one precise moment of time. That is why his paintings continue to give pleasure. Because they are devoid of anecdote, they enable us to share in the emotion created by a particular atmosphere. The impression of their being true to nature comes from the way in which the geography of a particular scene has been studied. Before Courbet, painters were above all concerned with depicting matter and space. Boudin, faced by the ever-changing sky above the Seine estuary, put all this into question. He had not been trained in how he should look at nature; he had no tricks of the trade. He saw everything with a fresh eye and an original manner. Faced with a choice between perfect craftsmanship, which was much prized at that time, and the rendering of immediate impressions, he opted for the latter. The images he captures on canvas are fleeting, suspended in time for one brief instant. Even his technique seems hurried, as if he were afraid of seeing his subject disappear. Creating an atmosphere is all that matters, even if this means the appearance of clumsiness. If one can see the brushstrokes, it is because they convey an impression of wind. If colours run over the outlines of a shape, it is because between Le Havre and Deauville the light is saturated with sea-spray; shapes dissolve, blurr, and become mere blots of colour. The minute droplets of water suspended in the air act like a prism and multiply the number of shades to be found in even the most subtle of tones. Paintings of certain beaches and fields, bathed in sunlight, emphasise this phenomenon. Sand, sky and sea and grass are no more than a reverberating mass of reflections, punctuated by the colourful vibrant forms of visitors from the city and flocks of

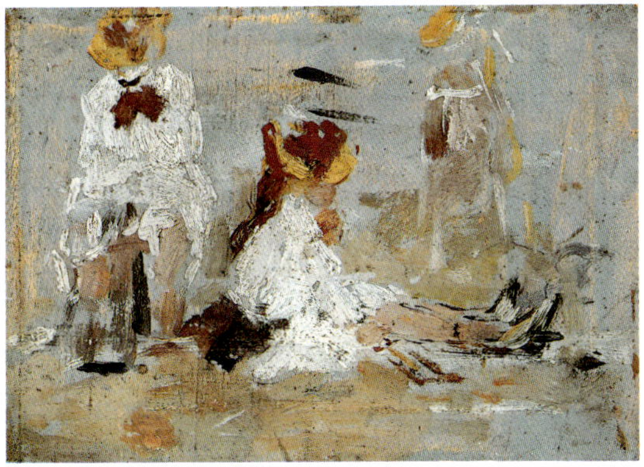

ON THE BEACH, 1888-1895.

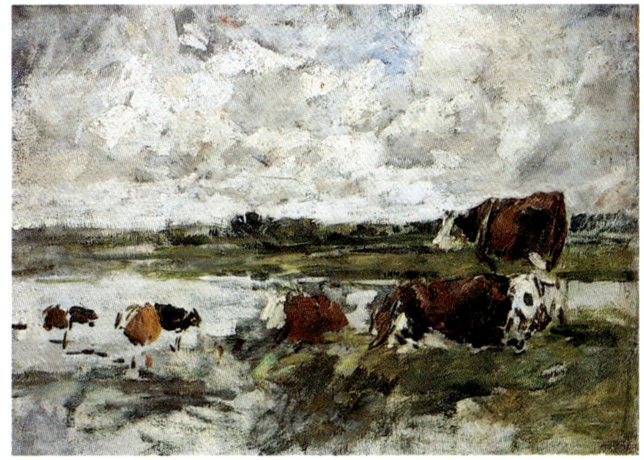

COWS BY A RIVER, 1881-1888.

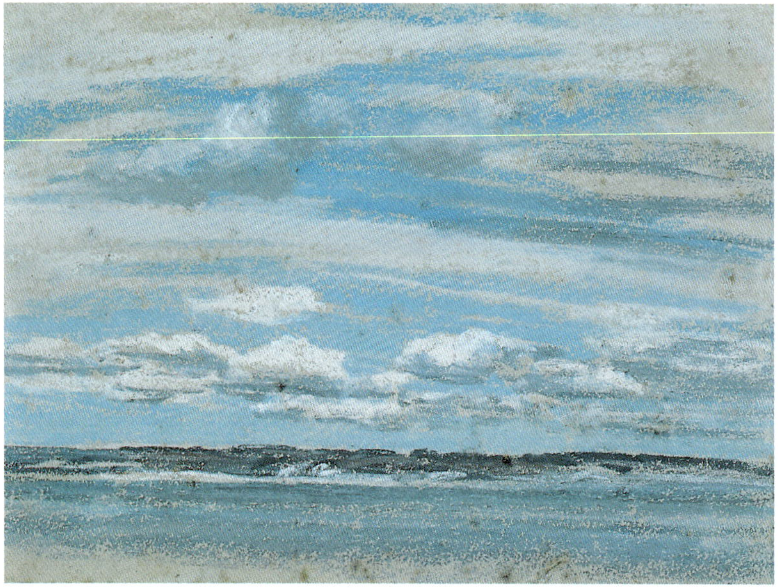

Sky and white clouds over the estuary, 1854-1860.

animals. This is why Boudin paints elegant women and cows with the same passion, dressing them in different materials (see p. 37) but making them shimmer in exactly the same way in the sunlight. The sea lacks any real consistency, becoming a tissue of reflections and wave movements. Like a shining pearl, it acts as a mirror to all things, including the sky which, in its subtle transparency, strikes us by its seemingly endless immensity.

In 1859, while on holiday at his mother's in Honfleur, Baudelaire, who was of the same generation as Boudin, remarked on his skies. He called his pastels, which had been conceived as a chronicle of forseeable or unexpected changes in the sky, «meterological beauties». Baudelaire had been a sailor for a time and was probably sensitive to the language of clouds, although he tended to look at the sky in terms of its power to stimulate the imagination.

Baudelaire's view of nature was that it was only valuable if it could induce dreams – or nightmares, since anything was more desirable in his eyes than the ennui of real life. «All these clouds with their fantastic luminous shapes, this dark chaos, these huge, superimposed pink and green forms that are suspended there, gaping ovens, firmaments of crushed or torn satin in black and purple, these horizons in mourning, all these wonders act like a heady drink or opium on my brain and make my senses reel.»

The world that Boudin shows us is much closer to nature than Baudelaire would have us believe. But, with apparent sobriety and free from the constraints of outline, the solidity of matter and the trickery of perspective, he fills the world with an extraordinary diaphanous light. In 1858, Boudin managed to persuade Monet to share this perception of landscape when he set him to paint from nature in Le Havre. The lesson was well-learned, and the future Impressionist master attained one of his greatest moments of perfection. He thanked Boudin in passing: «I have not forgotten that it is you who were the first to teach me to understand and to see.»

Except when mentioned, all the quotes are translated from the words of Boudin himself.

PLATES

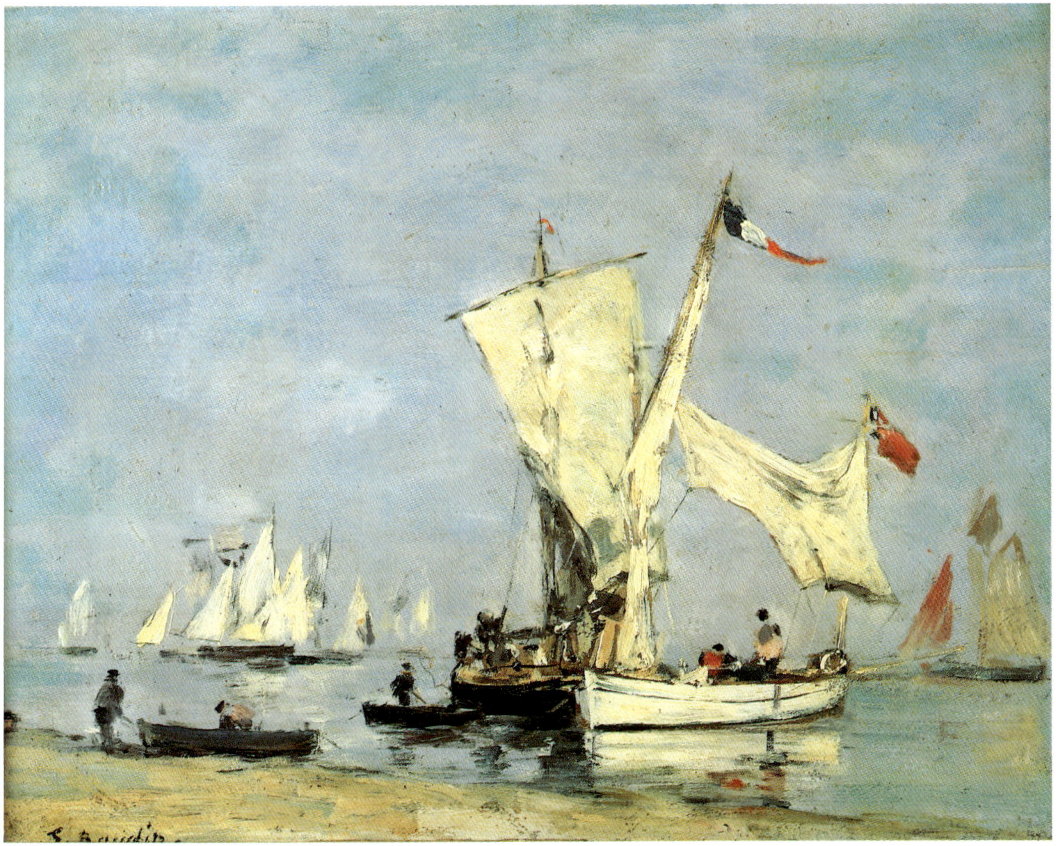

Sailing boats, 1885-1890.

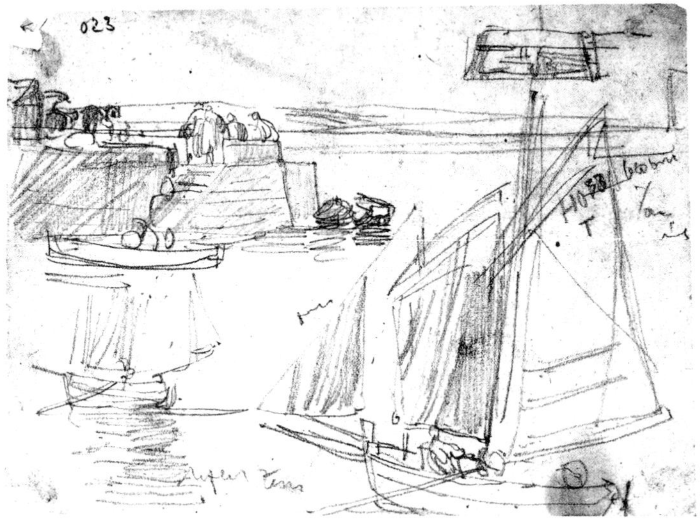

THE PORT OF HONFLEUR

1858-1862

Oil on panel, 26 x 37.5 cm, private collection

Above: graphite, private collection

When he started out, Boudin was quite content to remain in Honfleur. Like the Old Dutch Masters, he was excited by ordinary local events such as the markets, fishing boats returning to port or, as here, the arrival of the stage-coach. He made a great many sketches in preparation for possible paintings, but there were very few drawings which he re-used directly. The above example is an exception, and doubly so, for Boudin also treated this subject in pastels. The figures are striking in their lifelike poses, but we can already see that the landscape is given greater importance. The relatively soft and compact look of the clouds is reminiscent of pastels, which Boudin frequently used at this time in his studies of sky. Despite its rather unadventurous and slightly anecdotal aspect, the painting is impressive in the way that light is rendered with such freshness – a freshness specific to the Seine estuary.

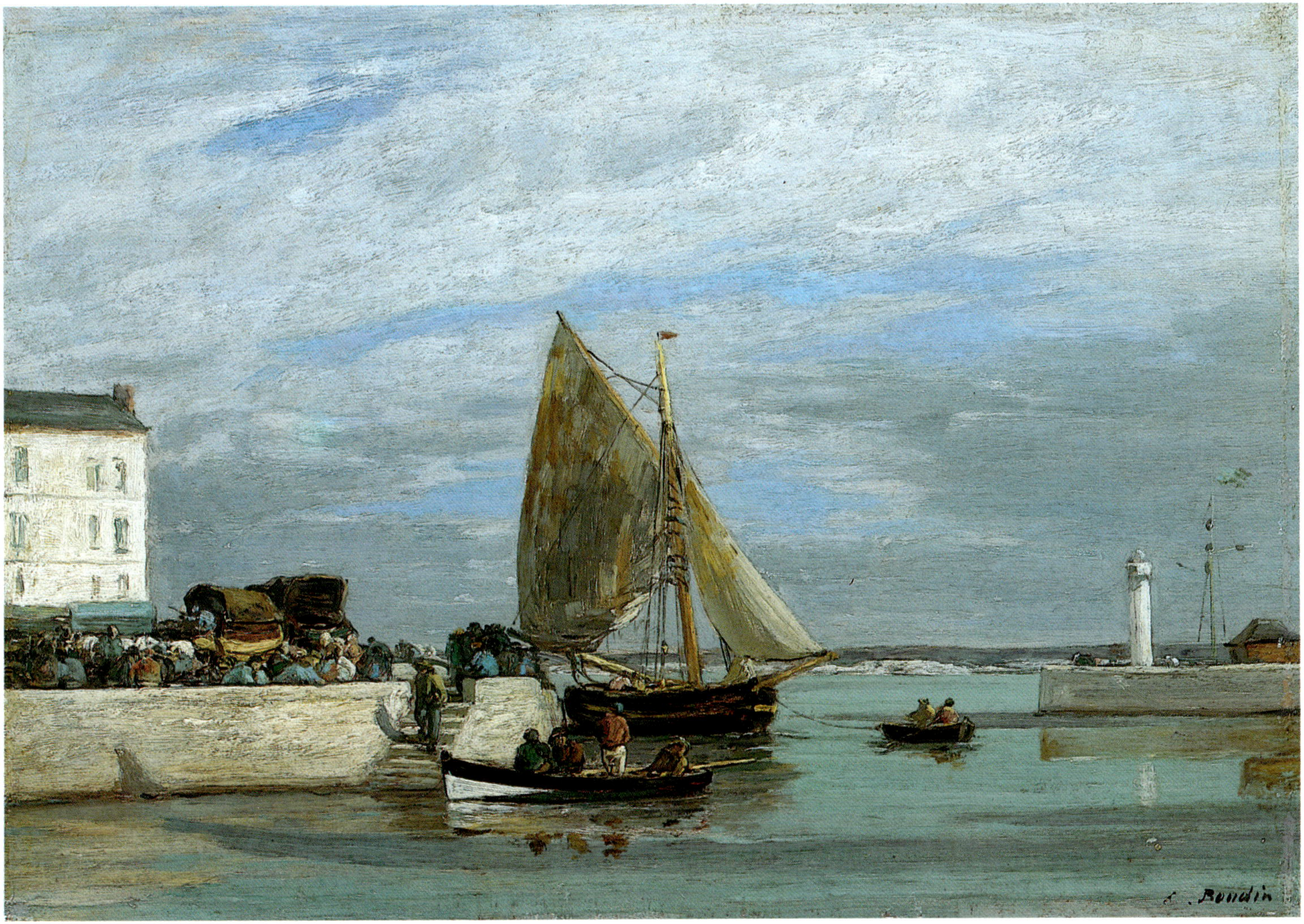
E. Boudin

THE BEACH AT TROUVILLE - THE EMPRESS EUGÉNIE

1863

Oil on panel, 34.3 x 57.8 cm

The Burrell Collection, Glasgow Museums

The expansion of the railways brought about the rise in the popularity of sea-bathing, a fashion launched in Dieppe by the Duchesse de Berry in 1824. During the Second Empire, it was Deauville that attracted high society and, in 1863, Boudin painted his first beach scenes. One cannot be sure who the figures are, as they are too far away from the painter to be identified.

Whether or not one of the figures is the Empress, this is a very attractive work. Boudin plays cleverly with colour contrasts between the bright dresses of the fashionable ladies and the more austere clothes of the other figures. The seething crowd of small figures by the seaside is bursting with life. In the foreground of this vast seascape, there is the anachronistic presence of a lamp-post, its top somewhat similar to the ladies' parasols. It brings a completely modern touch to this composition (with almost a foretaste of Magritte). If he hoped to find customers among his models, Boudin was quickly disillusioned, «We didn't get a penny out of our bathers this year. Oh well, I'll just have to be content with painting them.»

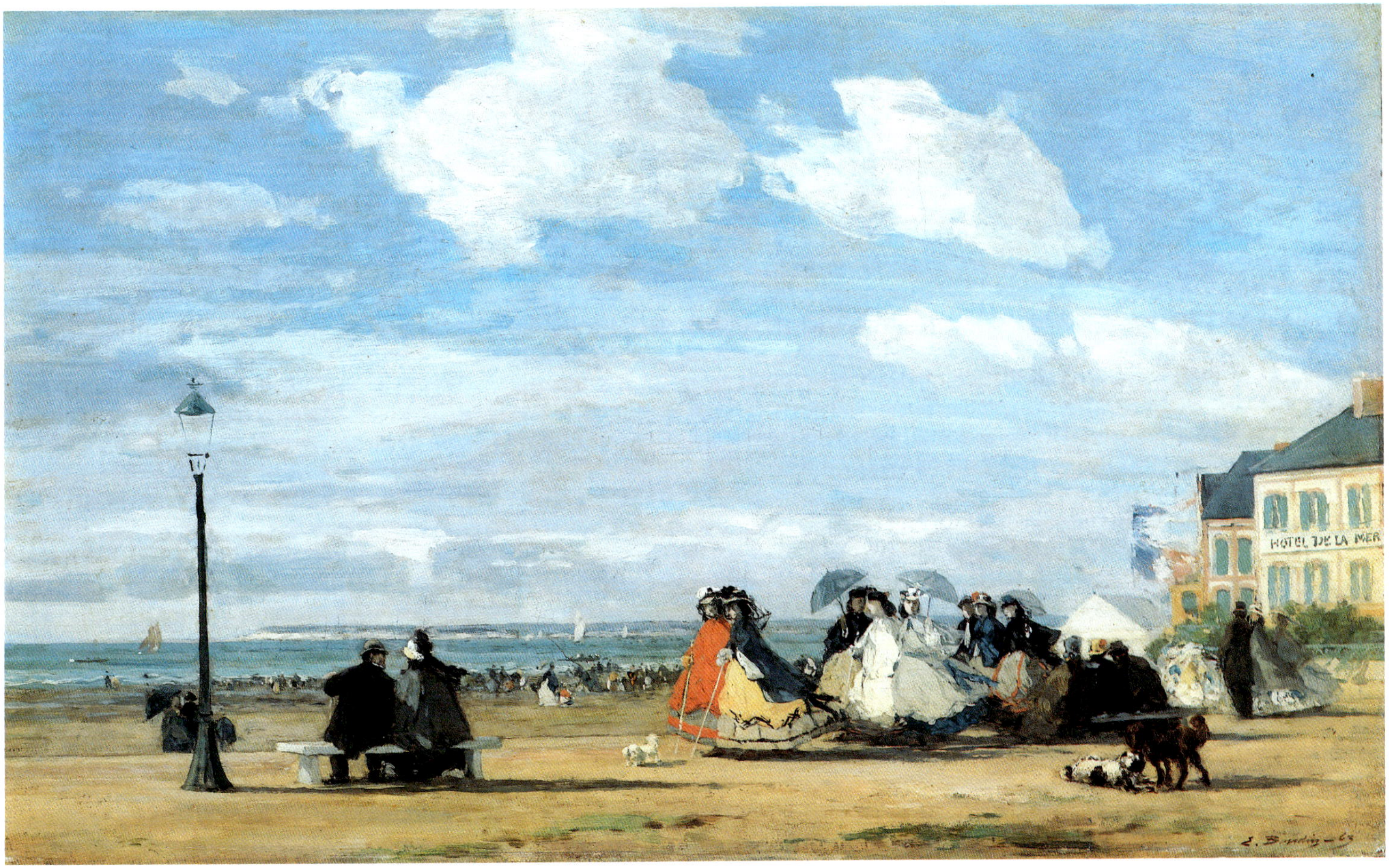
HOTEL DE LA MER

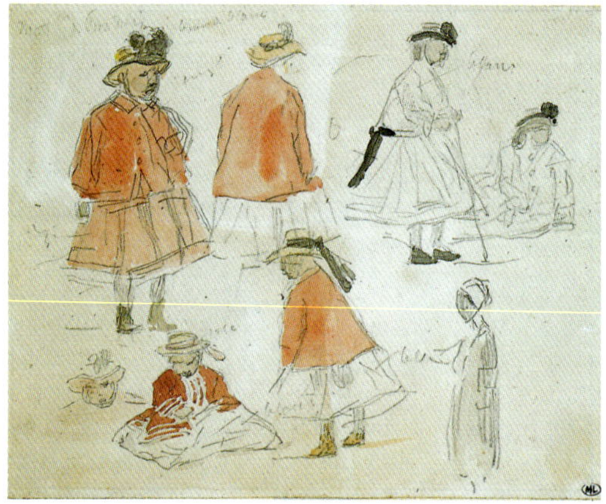

FASHIONABLE LADIES ON THE BEACH

1863

Oil on panel, 21 x 35 cm, private collection

Above: *Children*, 1865-1870, Louvre Museum, Paris

In certain beach scenes, the figures are there simply to animate the landscape and give a dimension to the space, a practice common with the old masters. Here, the small ghost-like figures in the background remind one of Guardi, whose work Boudin had studied at the Louvre. But Boudin adds a certain number of realistic elements (often from a water-colour study, as above) and typical of the beaches of the time, such as a horse pulling a lady's bathing machine back up onto the beach, or a small boat being launched. Dogs appear as a recurrent theme, in such true-to-life positions that their presence goes beyond the merely anecdotal. The two ladies in the foreground, with their coats ruffled by the wind, are not really the subject of the painting. Although they are an integral part of the landscape, the real subject is the sky which takes up three-quarters of the space. The impasto and the visible brush strokes enable Boudin to portray a stormy sky in the best possible way, and yet these techniques went counter to the predominant taste of the time, which was for seamless, highly-finished works. This partly explains why Boudin did not have a great deal of success with his contemporaries.

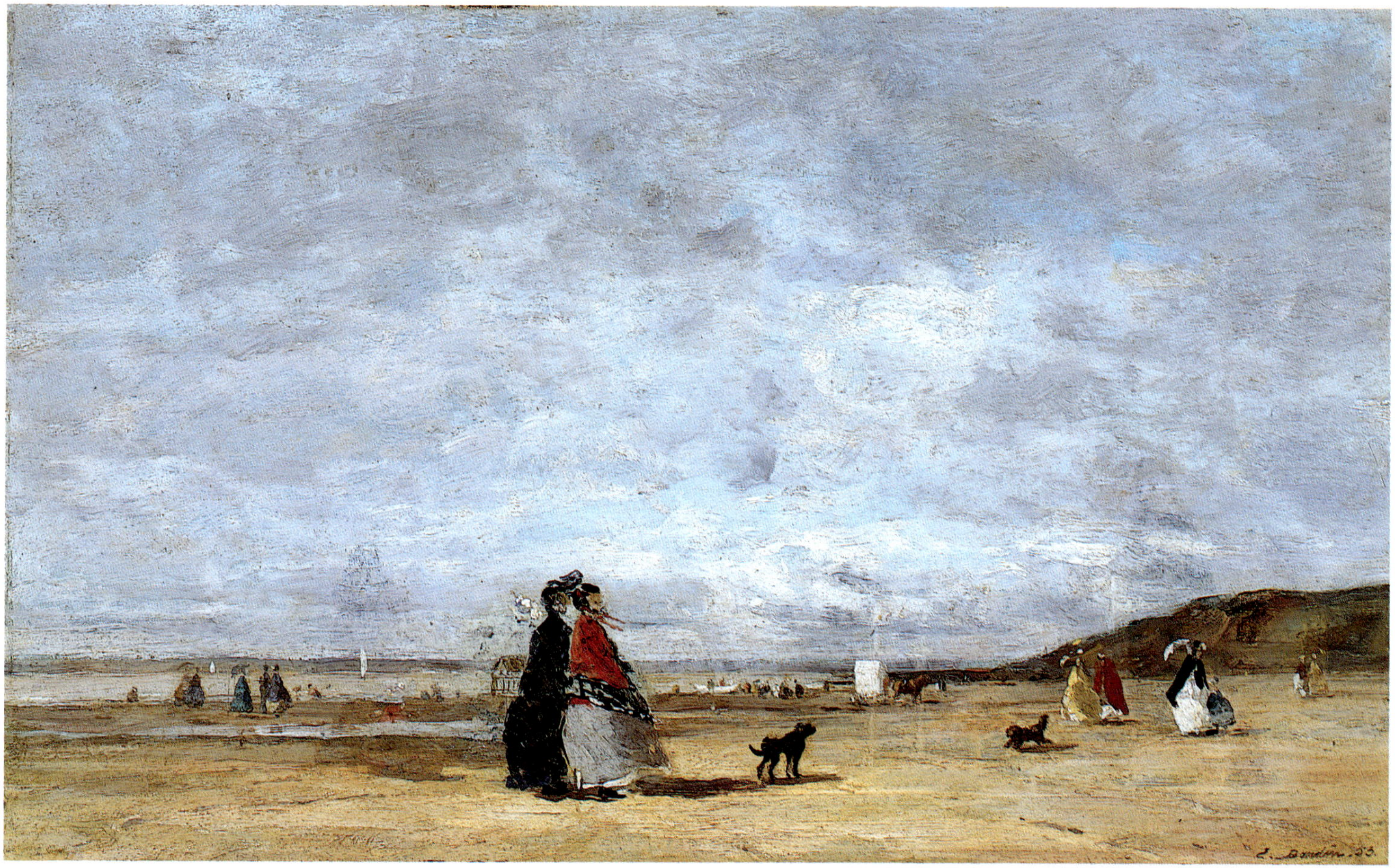

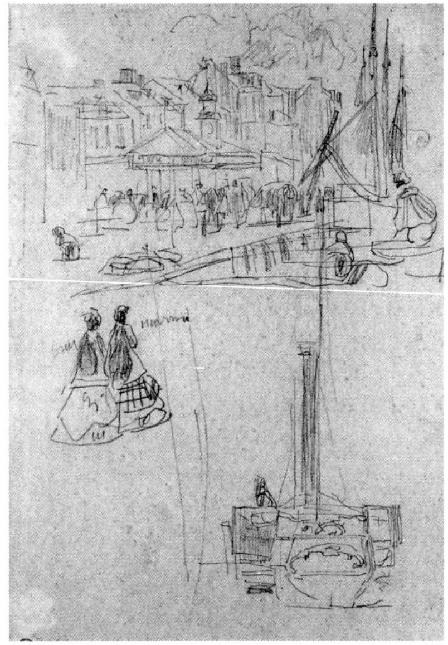

THE QUAYSIDE AT TROUVILLE

——— c. 1864-1866 ———

Oil on panel, 27 x 38 cm, private collection

Above: graphite, Louvre Museum, Paris

In 1852, Flaubert deplored the changes in Trouville: «But it has been changed, quite changed, our poor Trouville. The last time I went there, five years ago, I could hardly recognise it for it had been spoiled by so much embellishment, and by so many society people making it dirty.» Boudin, on the other hand, appreciated Trouville. It brought together the elements which he held dear. The invasion by high society, which inspired his beach scenes (p. 15 and p. 17), did not stifle the traditional town life (p. 39). As we can see, around the fishmarket on the quayside, fishermen and city dwellers rubbed shoulders. At that time, the port was important enough to attract boats of some size, such as the brig at anchor in the foreground. There was also the steamship which Boudin painted here and which operated a regular shuttle service to and from Le Havre.

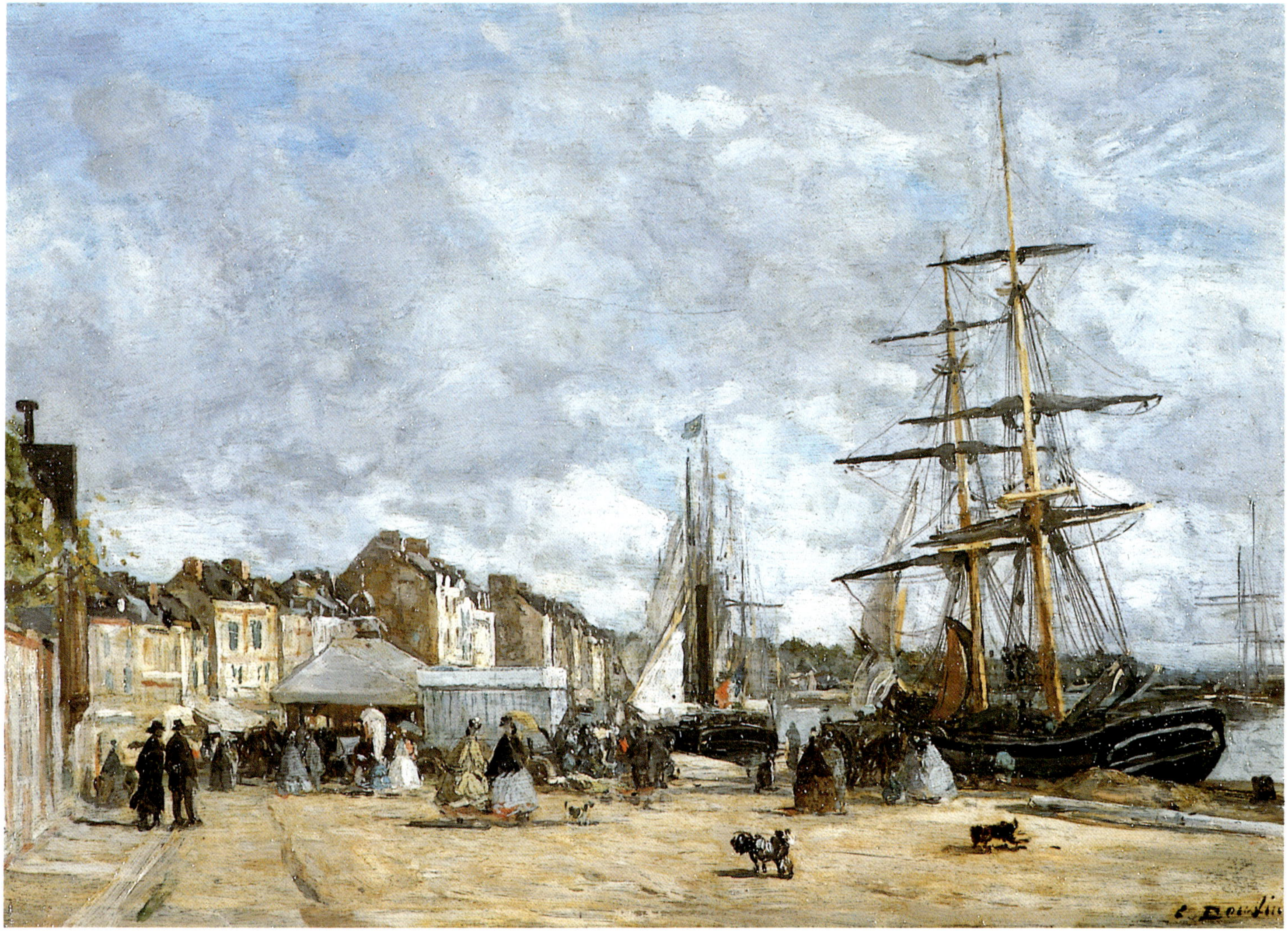

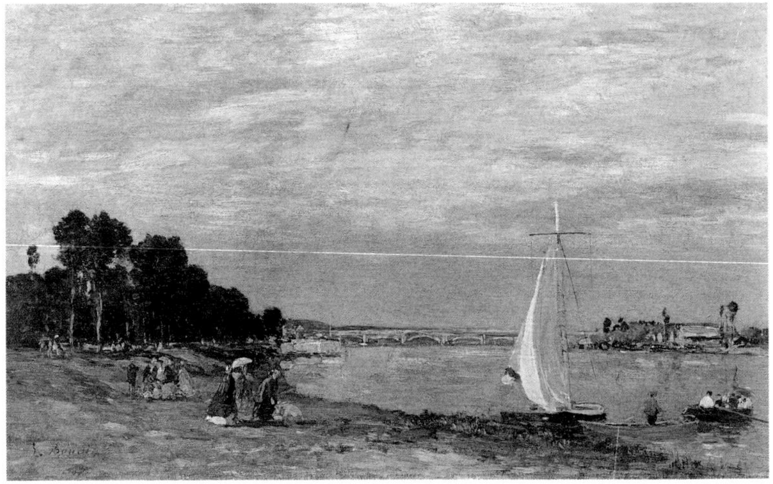

THE REGATTA AT ARGENTEUIL

1866

Oil on canvas, 46 x 73 cm, Art Gallery, Johannesburg

Above : *The Seine at Argenteuil*, 1866, oil on canvas, 29.8 x 47 cm

Collection of Mr and Mrs Paul Mellon, Upperville, Virginia.

These works are remarkable from several points of view. Firstly, these are the only paintings that Boudin ever did of the Paris area. Even though he spent all his winters in the capital, Boudin, unlike the Impressionists, never painted a view of the city – its importance in the art world meant far more to him than its beauty: «This devilish city of Paris is truly the only city where one can develop one's faculties. At every step, there is someone there to push you forward and make you progress.» Boudin went to Argenteuil to paint the basin and the regatta six years before Monet did. In his composition, Boudin contrasts the banks of the basin, rippling with its dense crowd and reminding us of the beach scenes, with the bright river Seine and the glittering white sails of the boats upon it. Boudin had never been so close to Impressionism, at a time when the Impressionists were still unsure of which way to go.

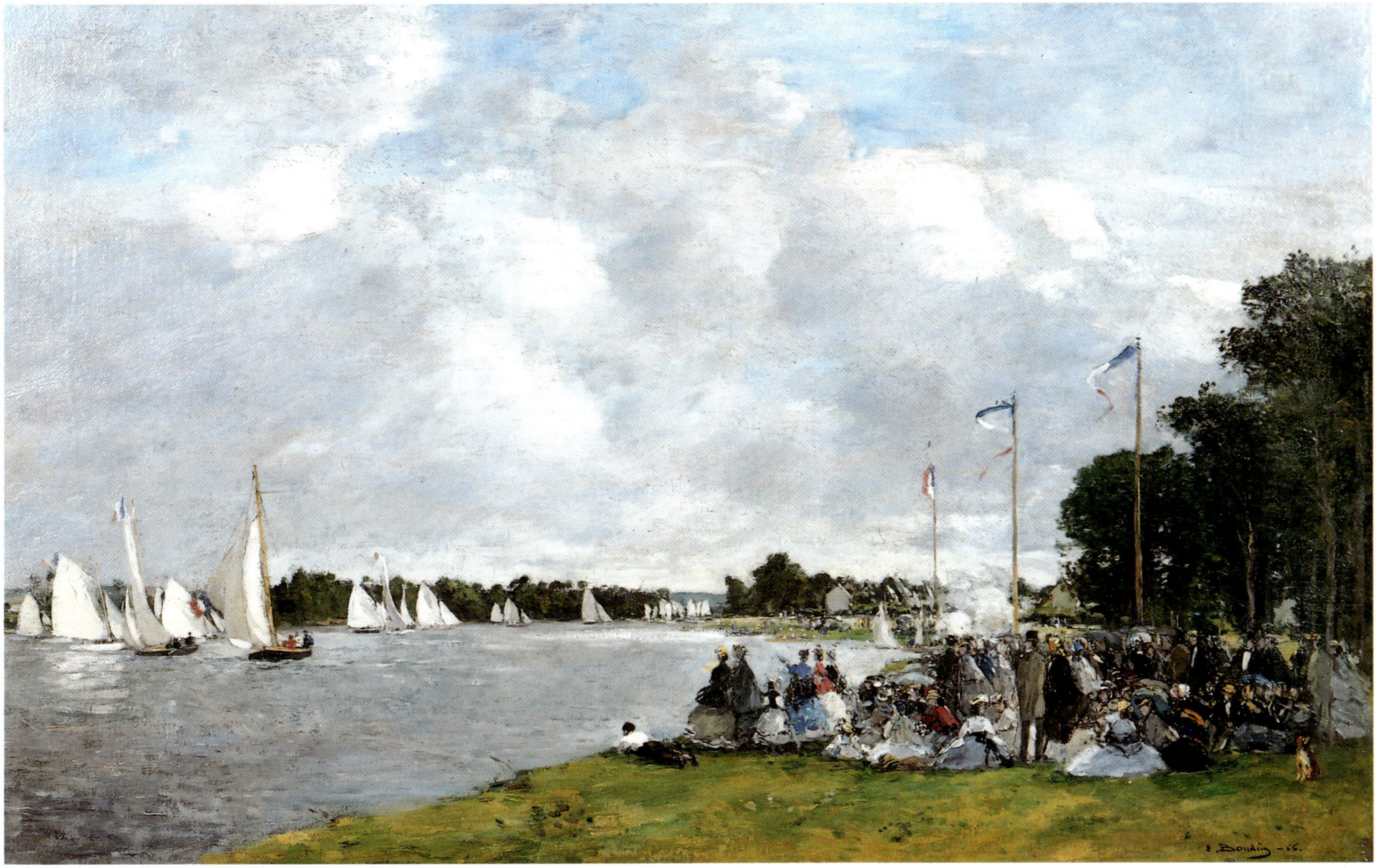
E. Boudin – 66.

THE ENGLISH FLEET COMES TO PICK UP THE SOLDIERS' REMAINS, BURIED IN ANTWERP CITADEL

c. 1871

Oil on panel, 21 x 27 cm

Eugène Boudin Museum, Honfleur

In December 1870, when most of his contemporaries fled the Prussian invasion and left for London, Boudin chose to go to Brussels to take up an interesting proposition. After several months in the Belgian capital, he went to Antwerp «to marinate by the Scheldt. [...] Views of the area are much sought after by local connaisseurs, so the orders come rolling in and prices are quite good.» This sketch, for a painting dated August 1871, is exceptional in Boudin's work in that it evokes a historical event. It is the taking of Antwerp by Wellington in 1814, an episode which coincided with the fall of Napoleon. It was painted just after the collapse of the Second Empire and Boudin must have thought it a good moment to publicly proclaim his republican convictions. The real title was soon forgotten, and the work generally appears under the incorrect title «Regatta at Antwerp».

We can see that from this period – and apart from paintings specifically destined to be sold – Boudin was already very free with his style. The painter was obviously much attached to this panel, for he kept it all his life, before donating it to his home town.

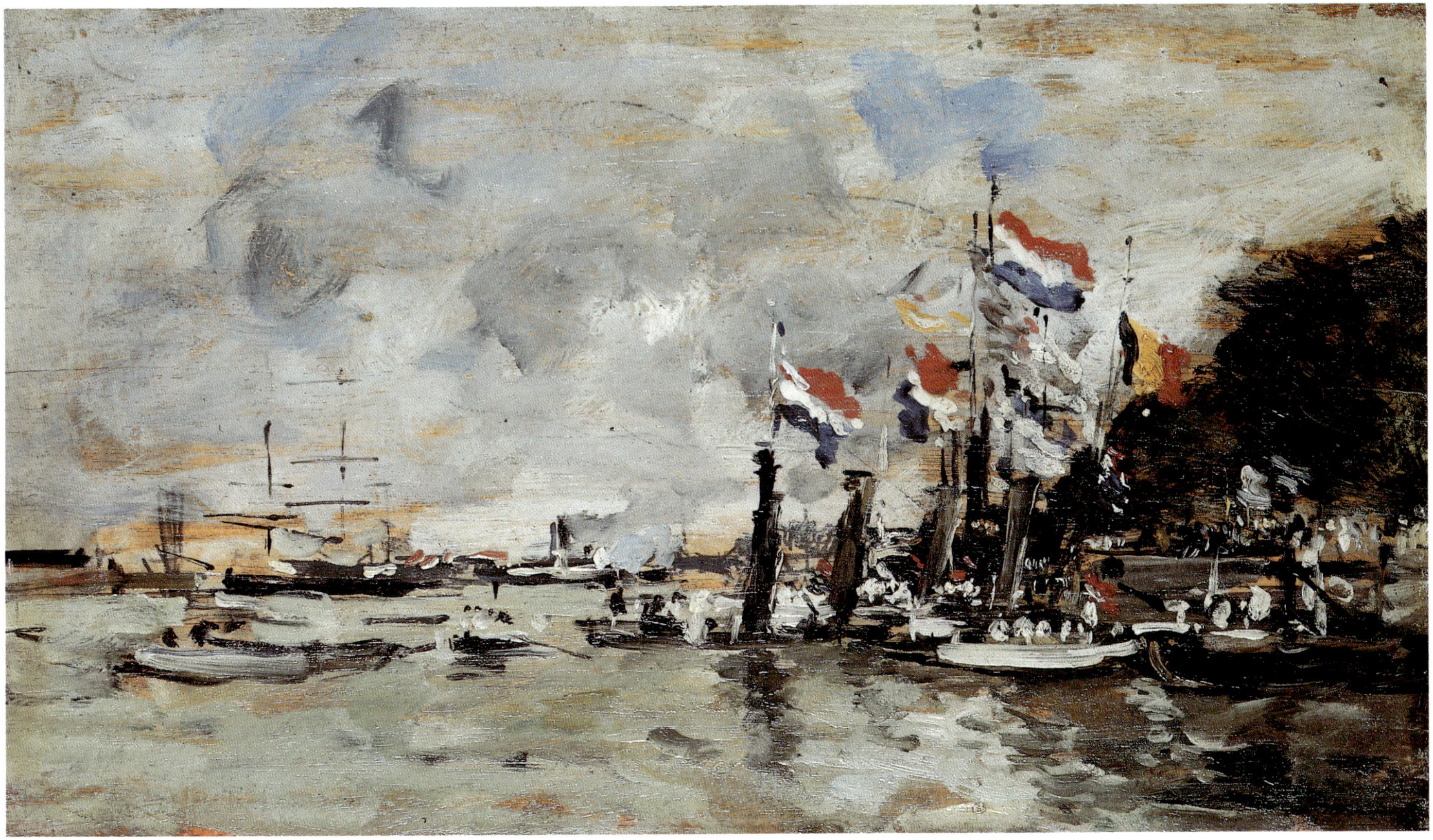

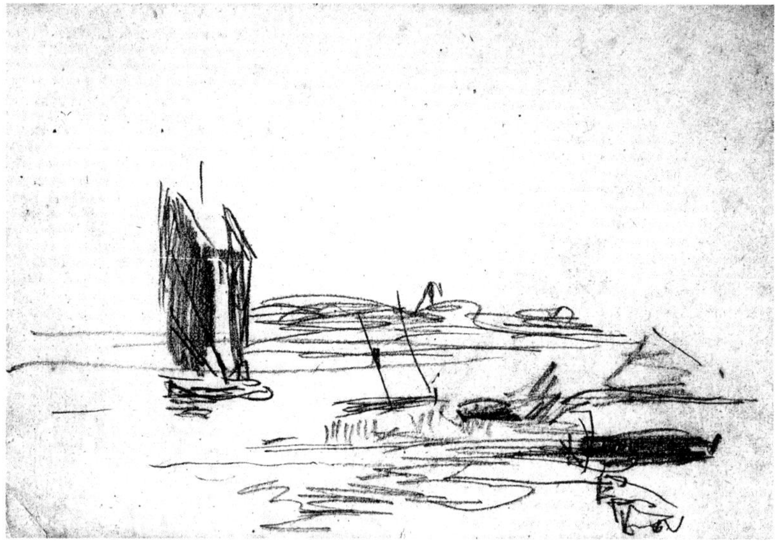

THE PORT OF CAMARET

1872

Oil on canvas, 55.5 x 89.5 cm, Orsay Museum, Paris

Above: graphite, 1865-1875, private collection

After a short period during which he developed a passion for rural life in Finistère, Boudin felt the need to get back to the sea and to landscape painting. In autumn 1872, he stayed for more than a month in Camaret, «in the shelter of the coast, with its little port filled with fishing boats and tramp steamers. Then its castle and its hill peeled free of trees where windmill sails turn freely. If a favourable wind comes along, you will see two hundred little sailing boats hurrying out together in search of sardines.» Autumn brought troubled skies, and Boudin, who sketched his canvasses from life, had to face «terrible weather on the coast where the wind is quite relentless.» He adds: «It was impossible to paint even for a moment between two squalls, and it was so cold that I couldn't go on any more.»

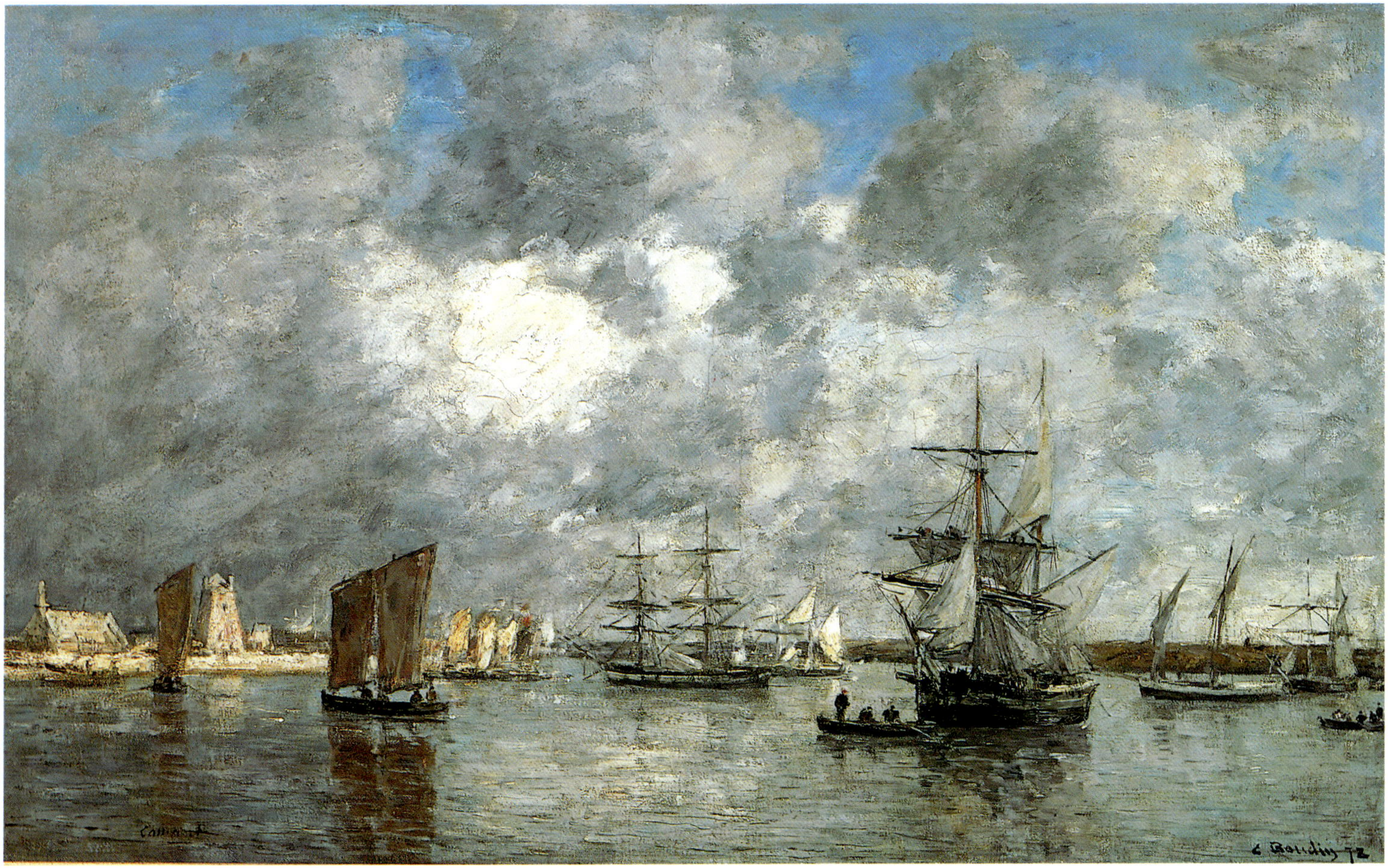

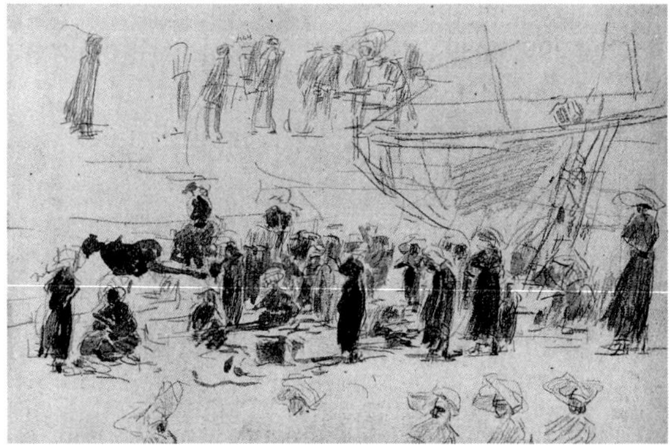

PORTRIEUX - ARRIVAL OF A FISHING BOAT FROM NEWFOUNDLAND

1875

Oil on canvas, 73.5 x 100.7 cm, Chester Dale collection

National Gallery of Art, Washington

Above: graphite, Louvre Museum, Paris

«We left for the North Atlantic coast where we stayed – my goodness – almost two months. There I had the pleasure of being able to work without too much suffering – and I brought back some sea studies which were sold in spite of the crisis.» Boudin was then fifty years old and the crisis he mentions hit the art market between 1874 and 1880, reducing his income drastically to 2,100 francs a year [about £4,000 of today's money]. Portrieux harbour was a gathering-point for local boats which fished for cod. They fished off Newfoundland from May to September, leaving at the beginning of Spring and only returning in the autumn. The threatening autumn sky of this painting confirms the season. The only bright points of this composition are the women's headdresses. The rest is dark, with the black hulls of the beached schooners giving the scene a certain austerity, which is doubtless what Boudin was aiming for. His father had crewed on one of these ships for a certain time and Boudin knew how hard and dangerous a life it was.

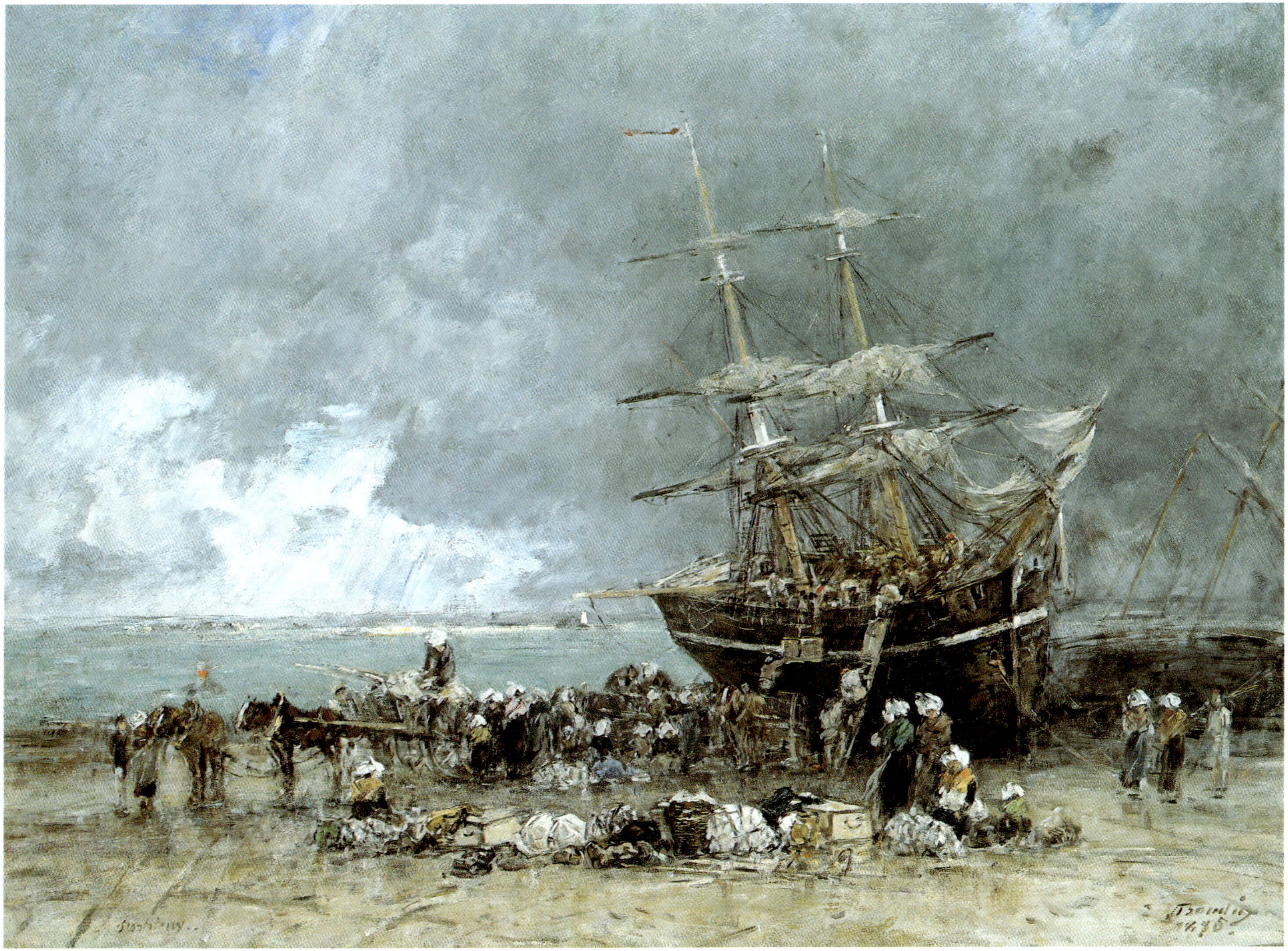

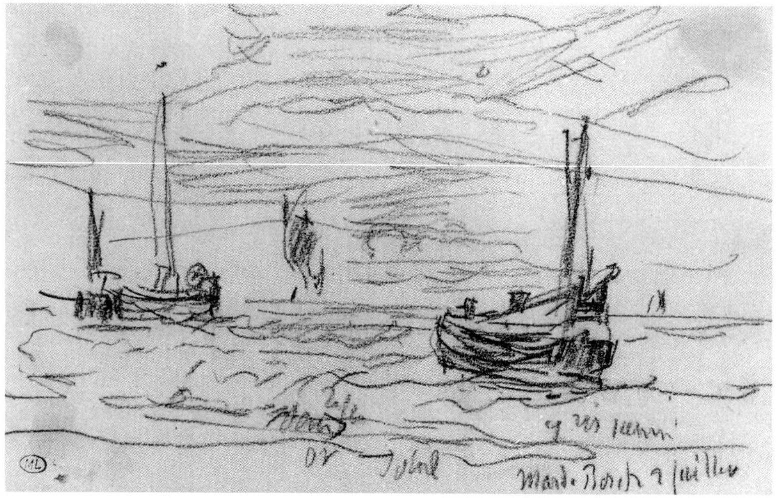

BERCK BEACH AT LOW TIDE

1877

Oil on canvas, 45.5 x 75.6 cm, Beaux-Arts Museum, Rheims

Above: charcoal, 1885-1890, Louvre Museum, Paris

«Berck is a vast beach exposed to all winds from the north, west or south; no shelter, just a few dunes, a large number of chalets and, below, some rather heavy, black boats without sails, beached up on the sand.» Berck, with its huge expanse of beach and luminous mist, so well portrayed in this painting, inspired Boudin for almost fifteen years. He painted its many facets: the dunes and the beach, with its fishermen whose pattern of life was dictated by the tides. Apart from this painting, which was probably exhibited at the 1878 Salon, Rheims Museum has two other views of Berck, done in 1890: *Le retour des barques* (Boats Returning) and *Le départ des barques* (Boats Departing). Berck was a favourite haunt of many other painters of this period, notably Manet.

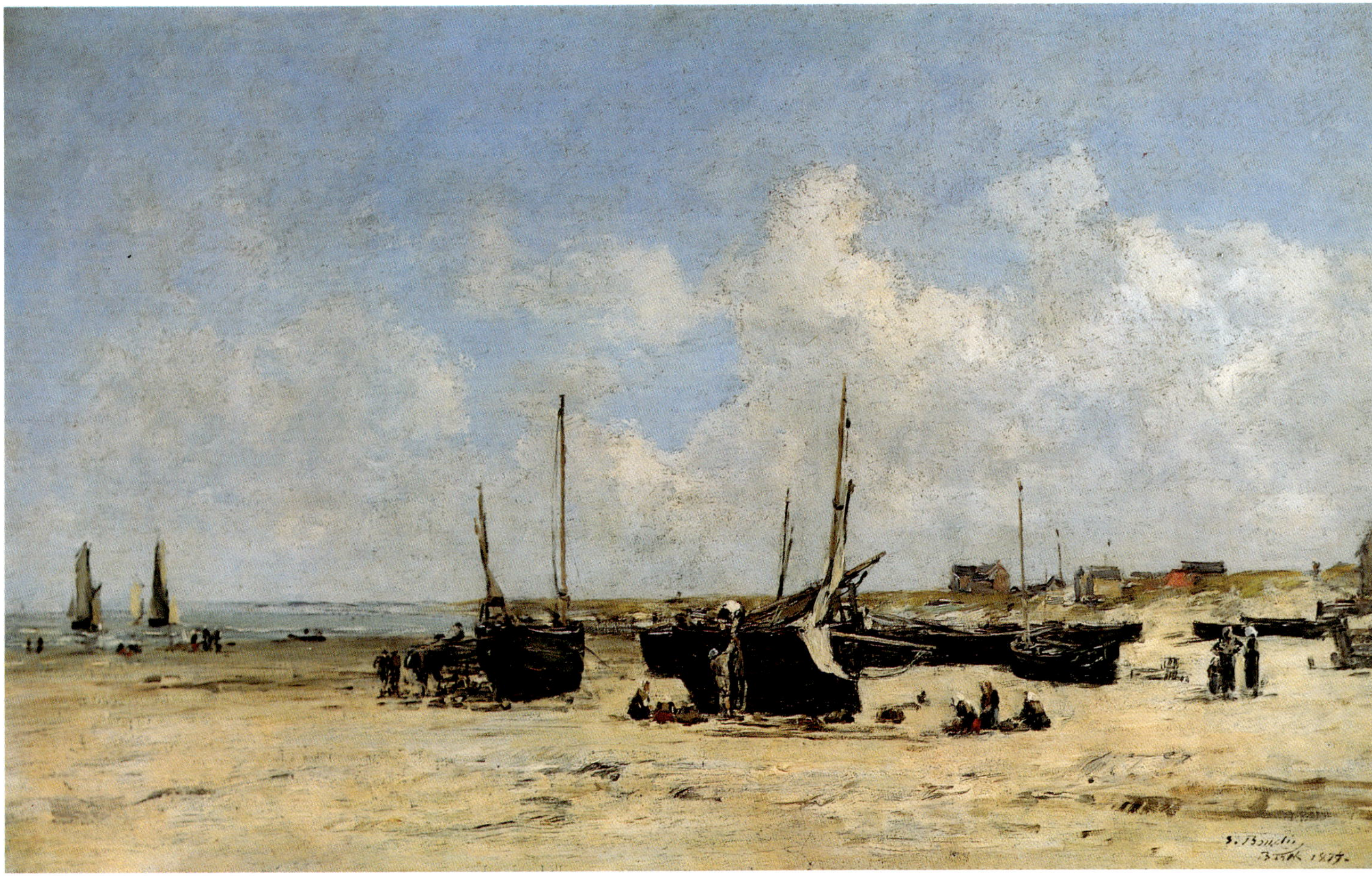

FISHERWOMEN ON THE BEACH AT BERCK

1875-1880

Oil on blue paper, 13.1 x 16.3 cm

Louvre Museum, Paris

In Berck, Boudin was particularly interested in the groups of fisherwomen whose characteristically red dresses are easily identifiable. His main concern was with the light, notably backlighting. By using chromatics and effects which blur the contours of objects, he broke with secular anecdotal tradition, inherited from the Dutch school of the XVIIth century (see p. 13). He also takes a fresh look at his own style: in the beach scenes with city folk, the human element always seems reduced to blots of colour. Here however, he is closer to his subjects and the figures have a strong presence. Boudin was to use the same procedure to paint his wife, once again on the beach at Berck. These two works give an impression of intimacy which is quite exceptional in the works of Boudin.

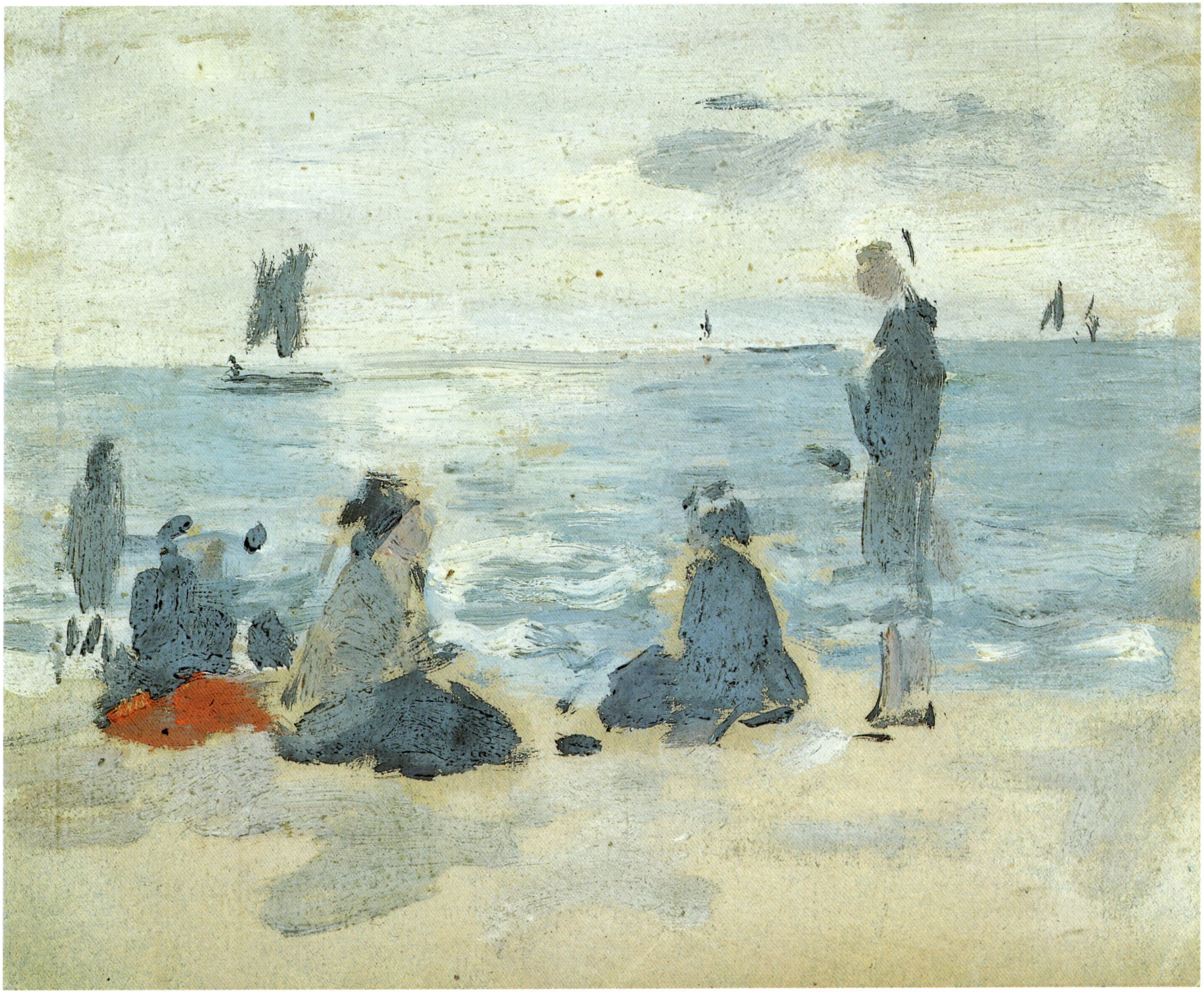

THE MEUSE IN ROTTERDAM

——— 1881 ———

Oil on canvas, 85 x 128 cm

Orsay Museum, Paris

Although familiar with the Old Dutch Masters, Boudin did not go to the Netherlands until quite late, in 1876. From this time on, he regularly worked in Scheveningen, Rotterdam and Dordrecht, by the banks of the Meuse. «This morning the weather is dark and rainy [...] It's Sunday and in this country of devoted churchgoers, it is not a good idea to work on Sunday among people so taken up with masses and who go to their temples to have some idiotic morality preached at them by yelping, tuneless vergers... Are we not nearer the truth when seeing the Meuse flow calmly beneath a beautiful sky?» It is this scene that Boudin portrays in this painting, exhibited at the 1881 Salon. Because of it, he obtained a third class award, called the beginners' medal since it authorised its holders not to have to submit their works to the judgement of the formidable jury. One might say it was high time, since Boudin was then fifty-five years old and had been exhibiting at the Salon for twenty-two years!

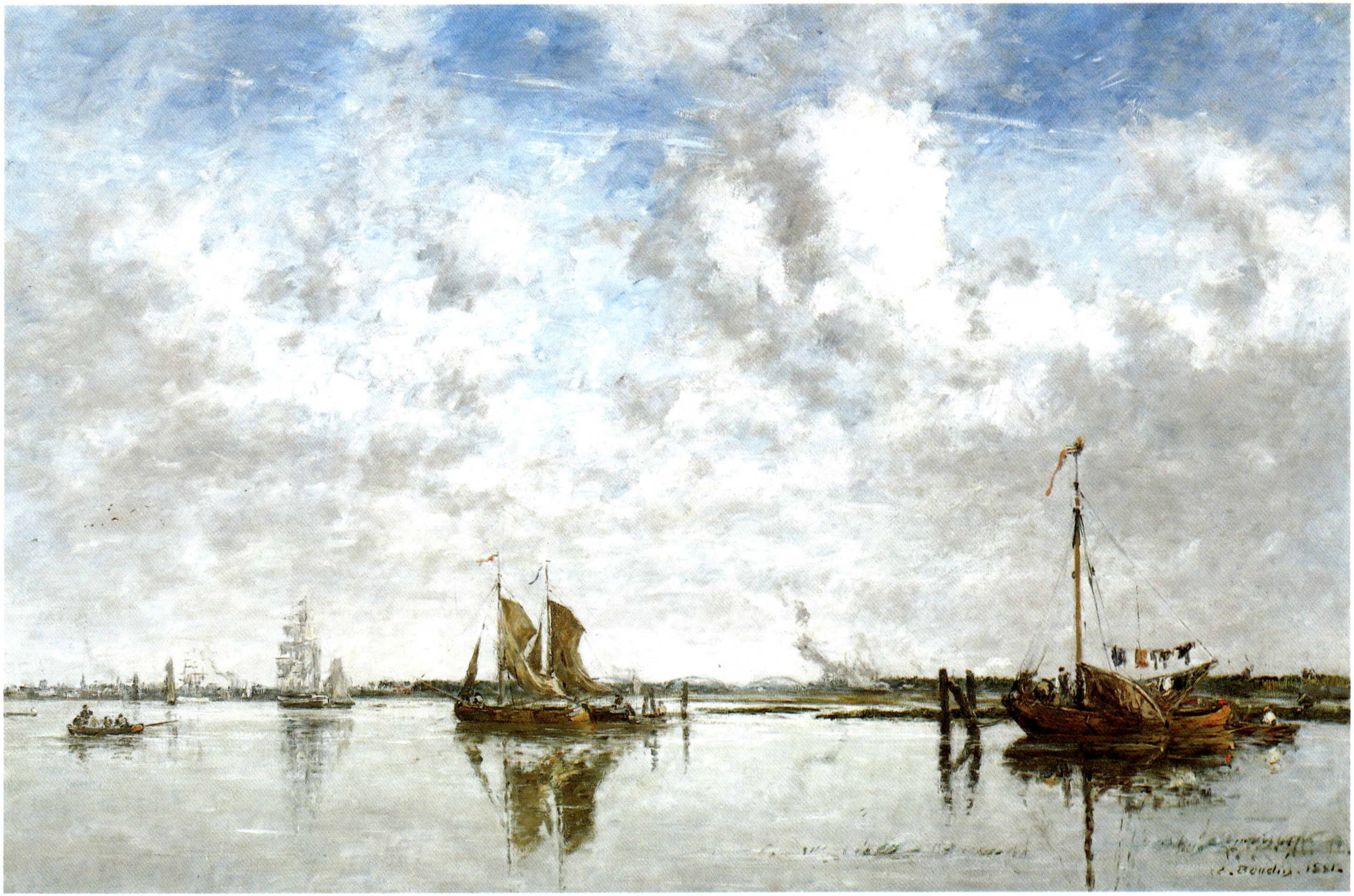

COWS IN A FIELD

c. 1881

Oil on canvas, 54 x 74 cm

Beaux-Arts Museum, Le Havre

«I have done my utmost [...] to complete my studies of animals. The sea has, by necessity, been neglected,» wrote Boudin in October 1881. He was greatly interested in old Dutch paintings, in which domestic animals abounded, and was at that time being advised by Troyon, the uncontested and much appreciated specialist of bovine paintings. It was therefore inevitable that Boudin should become interested in the genre. Furthermore, the Normandy countryside could provide him with as many models as he needed. But, ever the man of the sea and the coast, he rarely ventured inland. However, in July 1881, he went to Fervaques, on the outskirts of Lisieux where he discovered what he could do with animals on a canvas. «You told me about animal paintings and, to this effect, I painted a few, which in a certain way, resemble Troyon's, at least in terms of the subject matter.» Note the nuance of meaning with regard to resemblance to Troyon's paintings. While Troyon is descriptive, Boudin treats the subject from the point of view of the light. His shapes are treated schematically, to a point where the head of one of the cows seems to be a forerunner of Picasso's minotaur (*Assemblage : tête de taureau* [Bull's head], 1943, Picasso Museum, Paris) made of the handlebars and saddle of a bicycle!

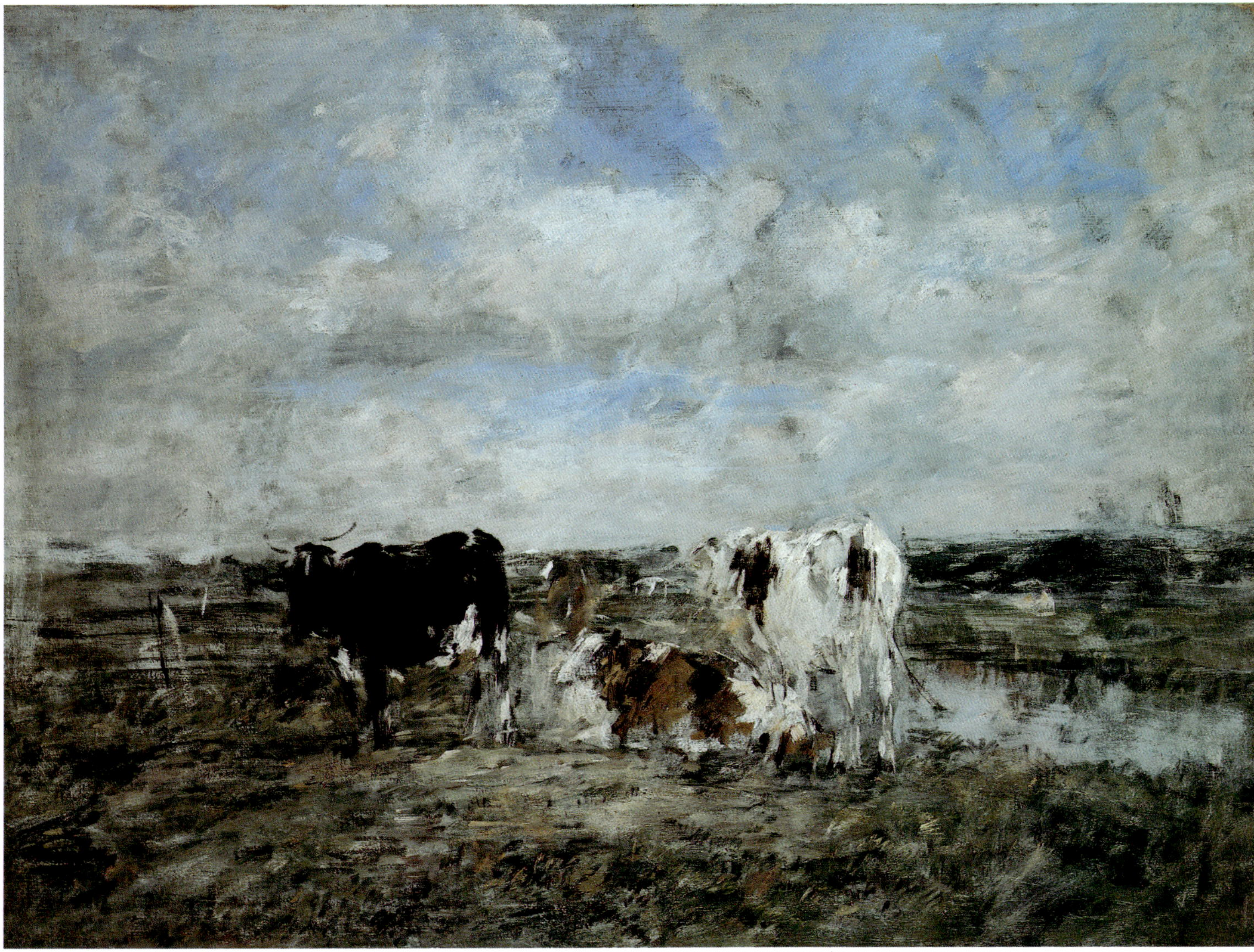

FIGURES IN FRONT OF THE TROUVILLE CASINO TENT

——— 1884 ———

Oil on panel, 22 x 42 cm

Eugène Boudin Museum, Honfleur

«No matter what else I do, I shall always be a painter of beaches.» This phrase, written by Boudin in 1865, was truly a premonition. His great production of beach paintings had lasted barely six years. His earliest known work on this theme is a pastel dating from 1860 (Marmottan Museum, Paris) and it was not until 1863 that he started painting the subject in oils. « People really like my little ladies on the beach, some say that it could be a gold mine for me.» But financial success was not to come his way and, in 1869, Boudin turned to seascapes. Beaches with «little dolls» made a comeback in the 1880s but his interests had changed and we can see this in the painting on the opposite page. The landscape is now less important than the figures and he has evolved from the disembodied puppets of earlier times (p. 15 and p. 17) to real people, who we can feel are flesh and blood. It is interesting that this childless painter showed a particular fascination for children and nursemaids.

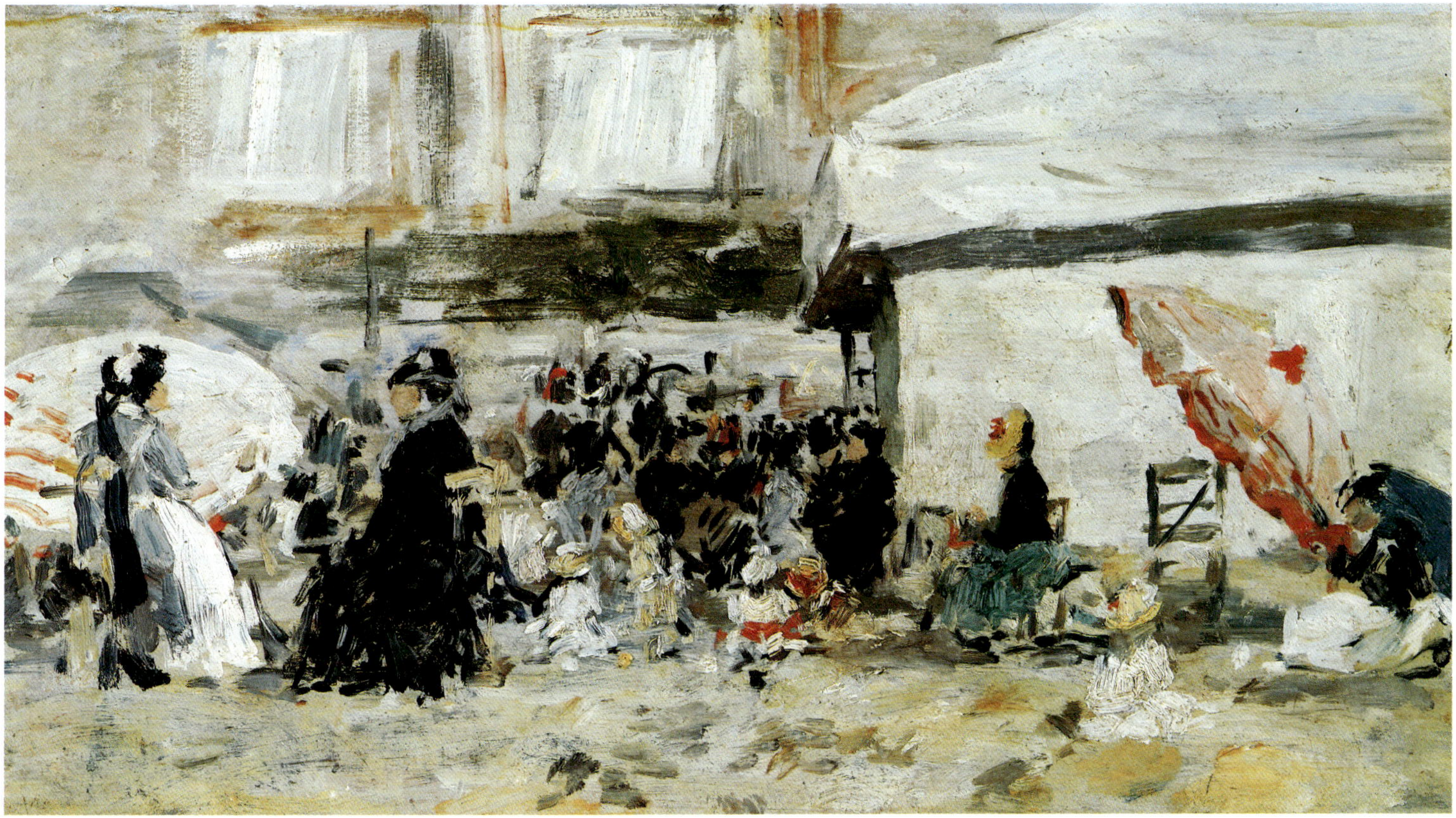

WASHERWOMEN BESIDE THE RIVER TOUQUES

1886

Oil on panel, 21.3 x 32.8 cm

Private collection

From 1885 onwards, Boudin brought washerwomen back to feature in his paintings. From the beginning, along with markets and fishermen, they had always been one of his favourite subjects. He was not, of course, the first to use this theme, so dear to Fragonard and Boucher. It is worth noticing that certain washerwomen still wore the same elegant straw hats of earlier years. Boudin's models usually came from Trouville. When the sea was at low tide, the fishermen's wives would go down to the banks of the river Touques to do their washing. The painter also portrayed the washerwomen of Étretat who used the natural springs which spurted from between the pebbles of the beach. Attracted by the billowing clothes and the laundry, Boudin treated this subject in the manner of a beach scene with city people, but going further in terms of style: sky, water and a few coloured blotches on the bank bathed in sunlight. Yet, despite the emphasis on colour, none of the details which typify the women's work are missing: they have their washboards, their aprons and their battledores. Even their positions and gestures are perfectly accurate. Boudin had a real gift for observation, making him a worthy heir of his much-admired master, Millet.

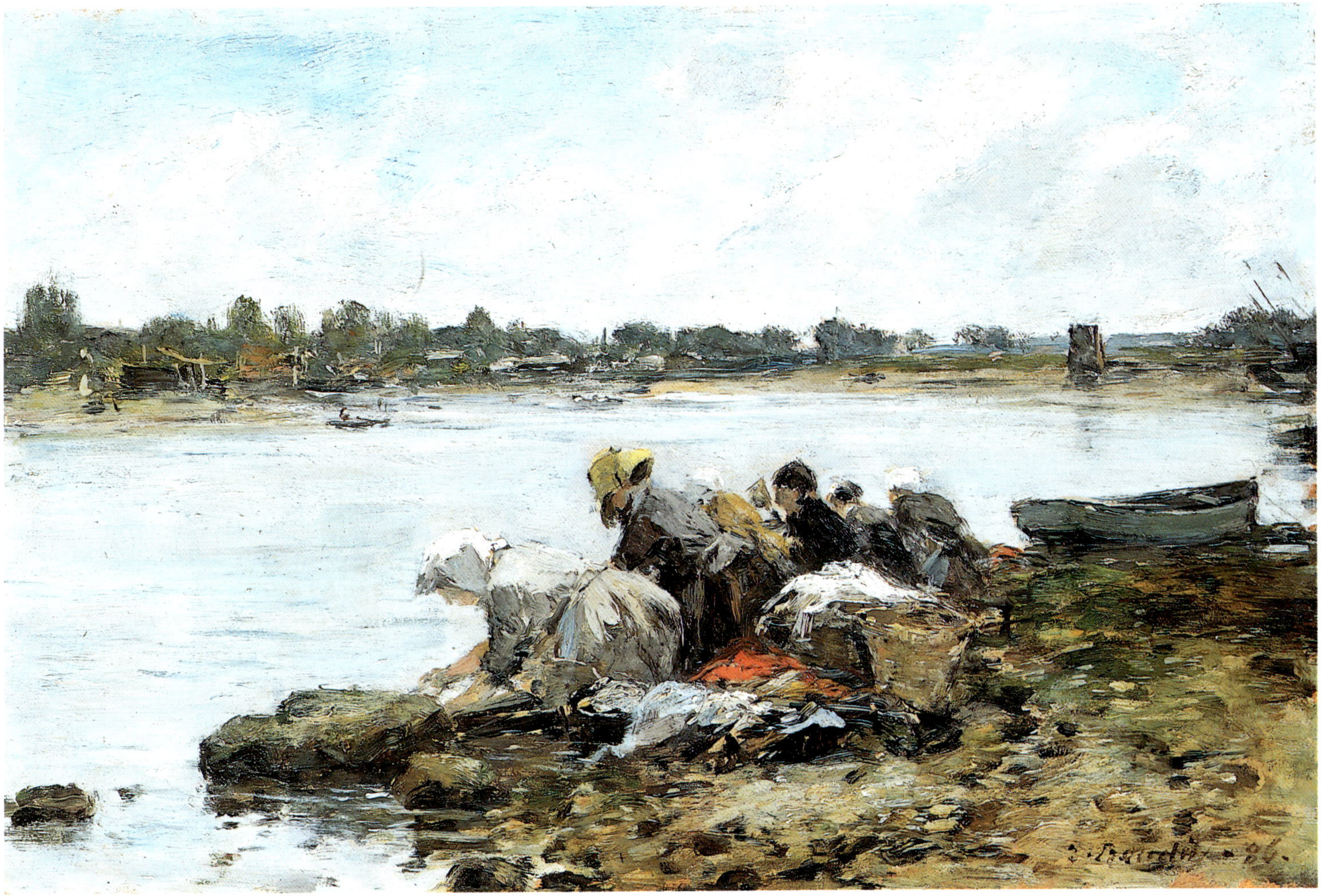

LOW TIDE AT ÉTAPLES

1886

Oil on canvas, 79 x 109 cm

Beaux-Arts Museum, Bordeaux

«We're off on an adventure [...] straight to Étaples but we do not know if we will stop there for long, it depends on how picturesque the countryside is,» wrote Boudin on 10th May 1886. Two weeks later, he wrote: «Stuck for almost a week now in Étaples in a hotel where all we do is get older. We would have left without unpacking had we not fallen ill one after the other.» His wife's health was frail and her illness gave him the time to do a few paintings, of which this is one. The sky is of major importance here, invading almost all the composition by means of reflections in the water. Baron Alphonse de Rothschild, a far-seeing patron of the arts, gave this work to the Bordeaux Museum in 1890. Three years before, Baroness Nathaniel had given one of Boudin's seascapes to the Rennes Museum.

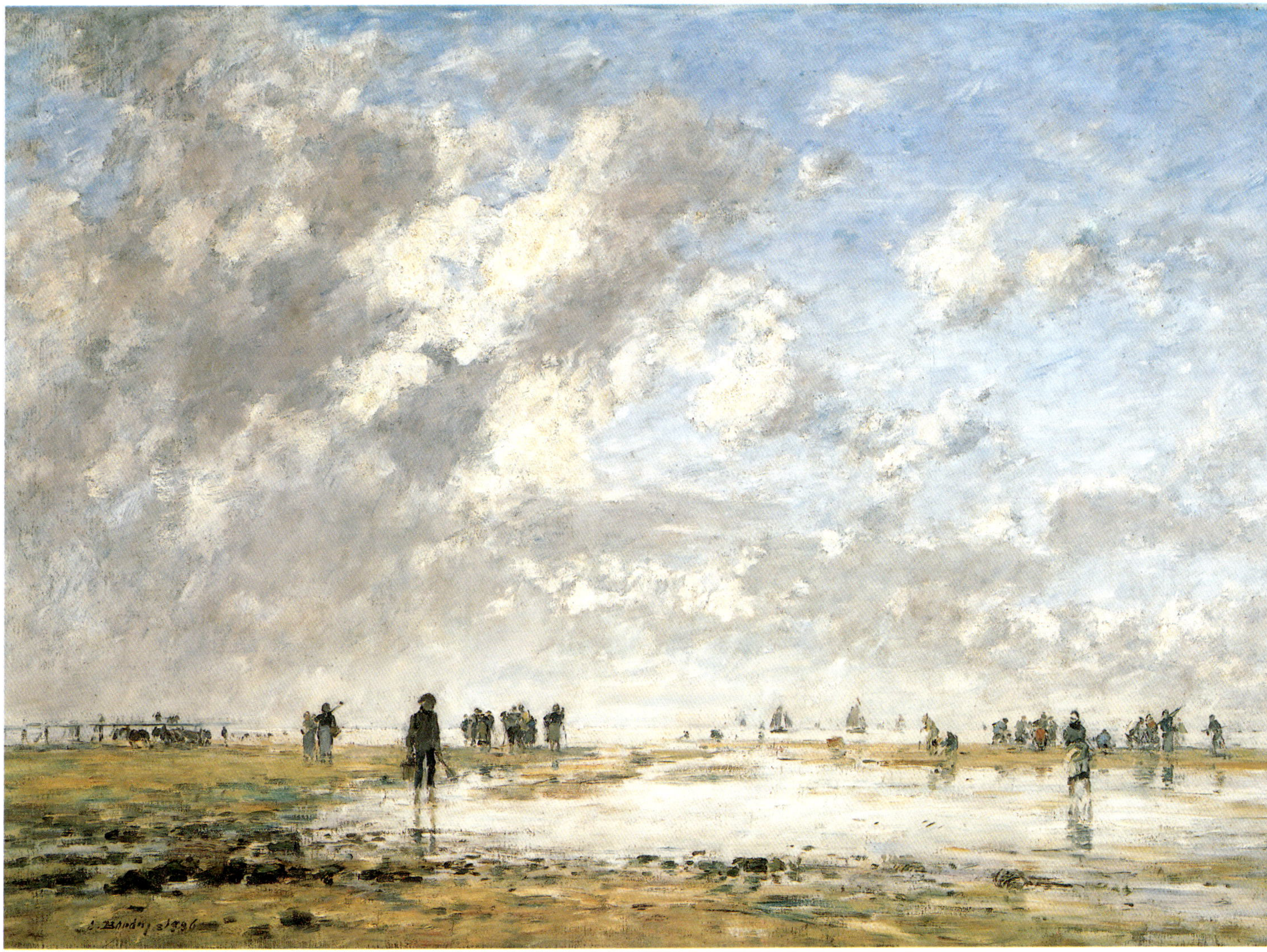

A SQUALL

1886

Oil on canvas, 117 x 160 cm

The Jacobins Museum, Morlaix

«Out there, beyond the dunes, the sea erupts in spray; difficult weather as in the painting: A Squall, from the Salon.» When Boudin wrote these words, he did not know that this work would soon be bought for 1,000 F (about £ 2,000) by the State, to be given – quite unexpectedly – to the Morlaix Museum. Two years earlier, the State had acquired (for 1,200 F) another of Boudin's paintings, *Marée basse à Sainte-Adresse* (low tide at Sainte-Adresse), of identical size, and now in the Saint-Lô Museum. The painting has some particular features: it is much bigger than his usual paintings, it is painted in an unadventurous style, and it makes a few concessions to the formal taste of the time. Boudin preferred the portrayal of nature when it was being more affable, and rarely painted storm scenes. Here, the unusual cloud formation makes the composition seem somewhat fantastical.

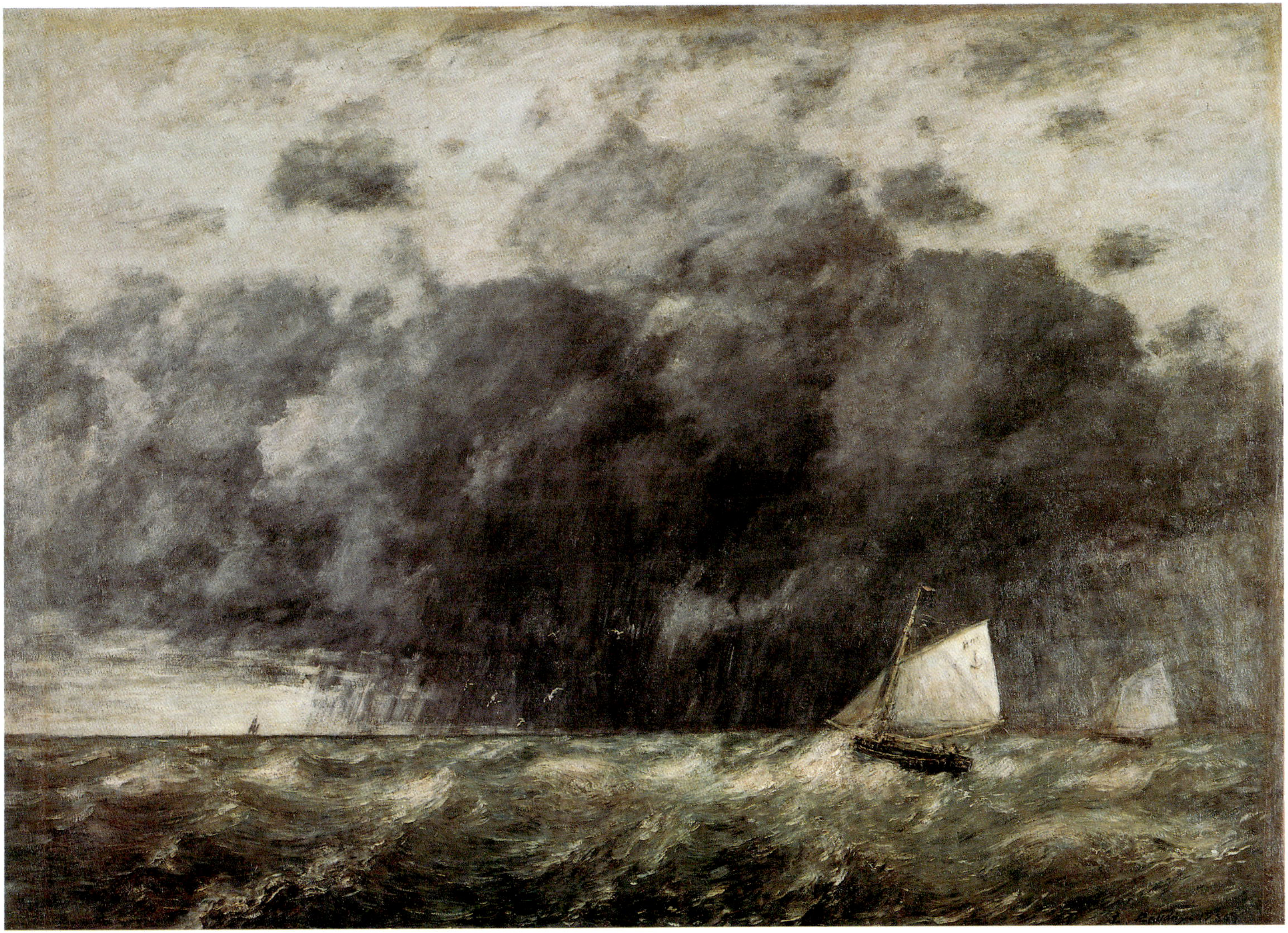

TROUVILLE JETTY AT LOW TIDE

1888

Oil on canvas, 32.5 x 41 cm

The National Gallery, London

«It is the end of the season at Trouville. This poor place has now been abandoned by sailing boats; we have not seen a single one for two months. That is what has affected me most – the slow disappearance of the sailing boat – which is already scarce – will make the sea a very monotonous place. How can I possibly paint these fat, heavy, shapeless iron boilers without sails.» This was written in 1893 and expresses Boudin's disappointment in the changes in a place he loved greatly (p. 19). Henceforth, he was to turn his attention towards sea and sky. «There still remains the sky which no one can spoil... not even the rancid smoke of the steamers... and the sea so fresh and lively.» In this painting, Boudin played on the contrast between the river Touques, with its mirror-like gleaming stillness, and what one imagines to be a windy sky. Beyond this, like theatre scenery, are the jetties and the spray of a rough, vigorous sea.

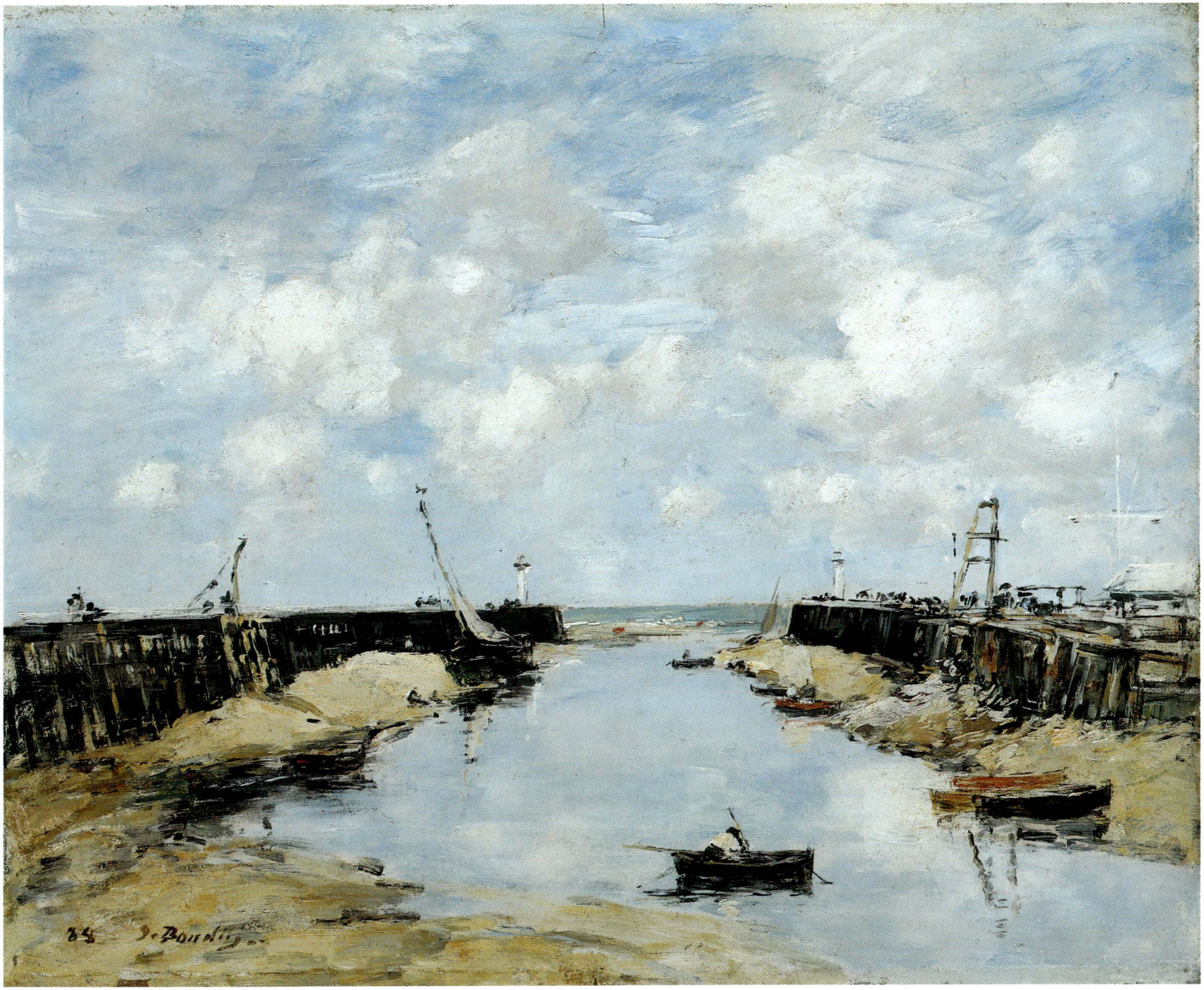

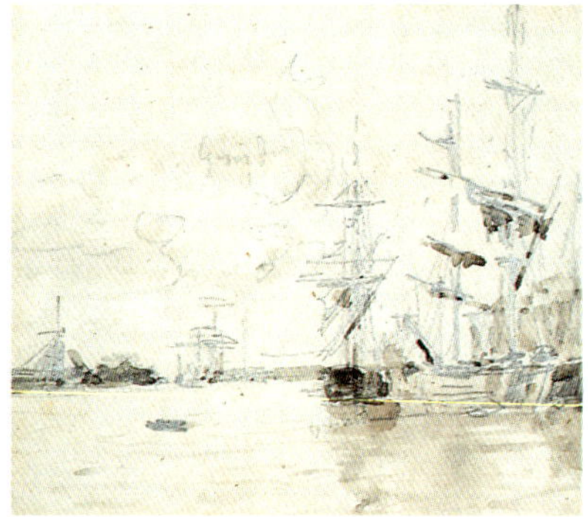

THE OUTER HARBOUR OF LE HAVRE

——— 1889 ———

Oil on panel, 26.5 x 35 cm, private collection

Above: graphite and watercolour, 1863-1869, private collection

«When I went into my room, the harbour under my window and the air up to and over the roofs was entirely filled by the brownish smoke of the steamships. Great clouds of this smoke mix with the jets of white steam which whistle up from the exhaust of the engines.» This description was written by Stendhal in 1838, at a time when Le Havre was just beginning to expand. One can imagine how it must have been fifty years later when it had become the second largest port in France. In this painting, Boudin alludes to its vibrancy which he knew well but did not really like. On the right, the thick smoke trail of a steamship almost blots out the masts of a sailing ship before melting into the golden sunset sky. Boudin admitted that he was a dreamer and here, in this painting, he shows himself to be the worthy heir of Claude Lorrain for, under the guise of realism, we discover a dream world. The François Ier tower, whose massive outline is visible on the horizon, gaurds the harbour entrance. A ship prepares to leave harbour, going through the mist towards a blazing horizon, evocative of an unreal world.

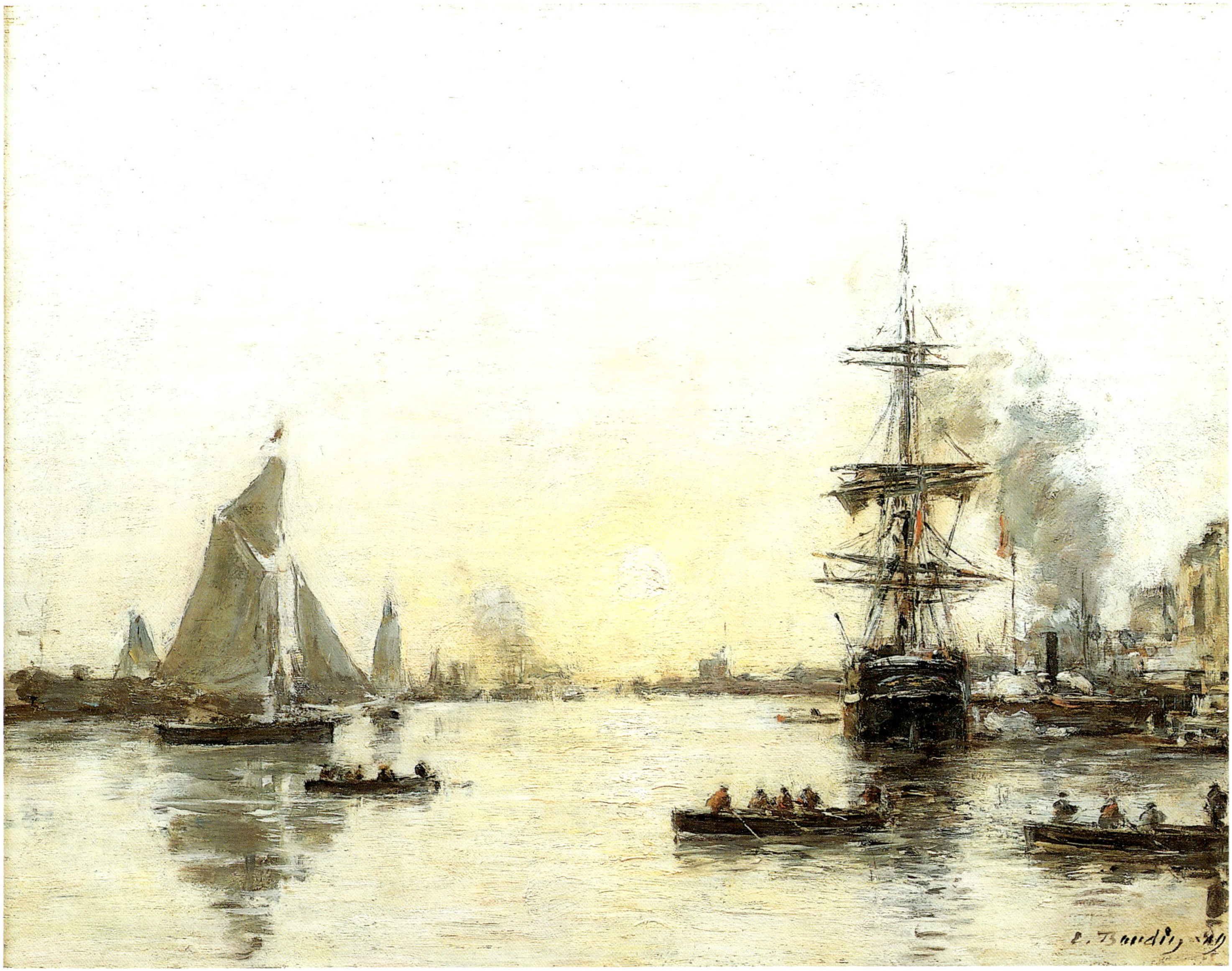

STUDY OF SKY OVER THE 'BASSIN DU COMMERCE' IN LE HAVRE

1888-1895

Oil on panel, 27 x 41 cm

Beaux-Arts Museum, Le Havre

Although he preferred beaches, Boudin also knew how to make the most out of smoke effects, closely linked to the development of the steamship. He showed that art could be produced out of a harsh industrial reality. When looking at this small painting, one is reminded of Monet's *Impression, soleil levant* (Impression, sunrise), also done in Le Havre but in 1872 (and now in the Marmottan Museum, Paris). There is no doubt that Monet's painting predates Boudin's, but Boudin's sketches for this, which show a freedom occasionally equal to that of his pupil, may have been dated too late by the experts. The painting shown here is proof of this freedom: an effusion of colours and a break-up of brushwork; the boats reduced to black signs like Chinese characters. But there was one major difference between the two painters: Boudin never dared free himself of certain conventions in his paintings destined for the public, whereas Monet treated his public and private works with the same degree of daring.

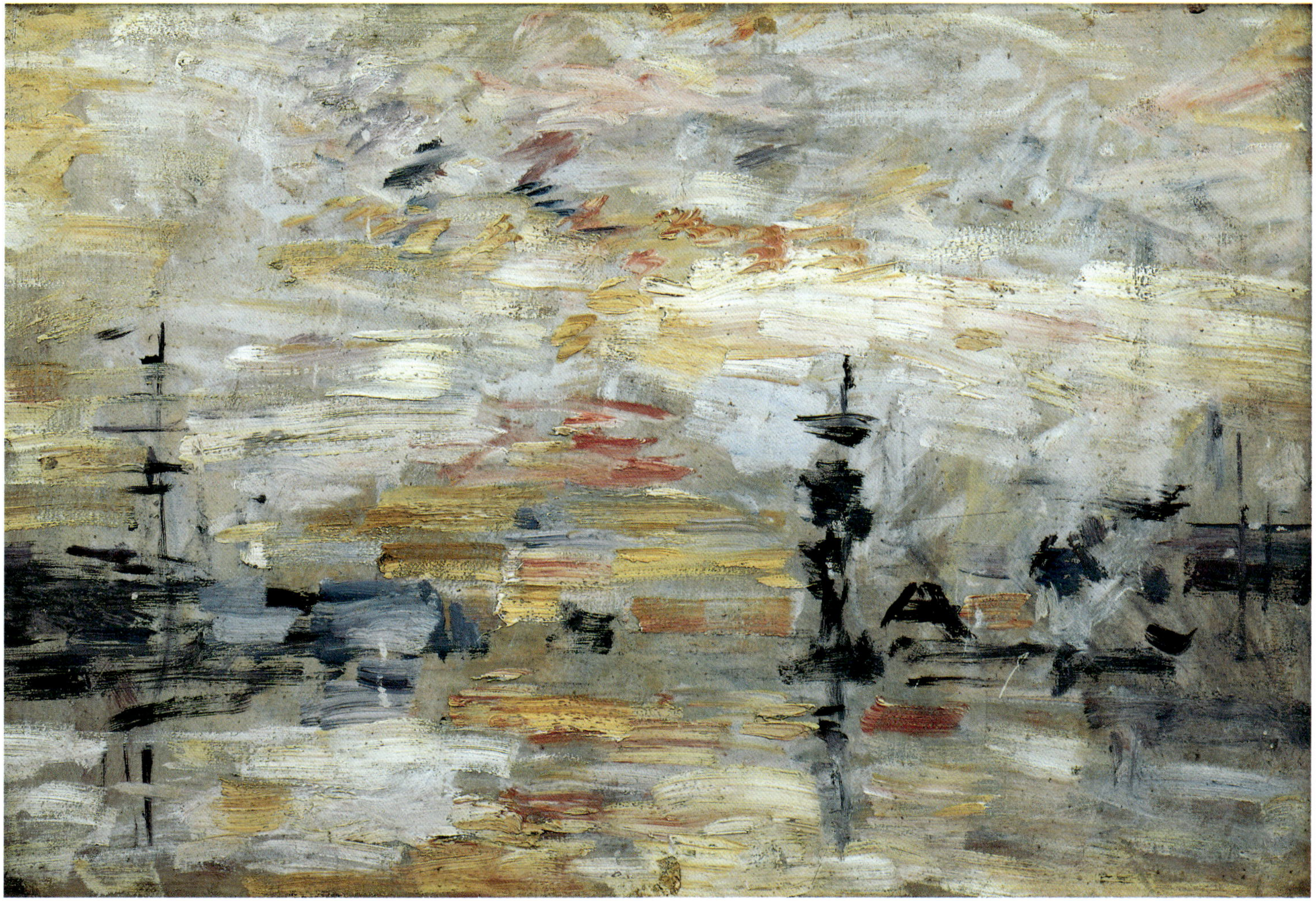

STUDIES OF SKY

1888-1895

Oil on panel, 27 x 22 cm

Left: private collection

Right: Beaux-Arts Museum, Le Havre

Before Boudin, studies of sky, devoid of any landscape, had been done by the English and by the French Romantics, notably by Delacroix. However, it is probable that Boudin knew nothing of this aspect of his predecessors' work. He only discovered English painting (Turner, Constable and others) in 1894. Furthermore, such studies were considered by the artists as highly private works which should never leave the studio. Boudin's studies of sky were done throughout his life and in different styles, which makes it difficult to date them. However, the objective «meteorological» studies that he did when he began his career (see p. 10) were gradually replaced by portrayals of brief flaming sunsets, in which colour almost took priority over the subject. He adapted his touch to the form of the clouds, not hesitating to leave certain areas blank, or only roughly sketched. Boudin was only too conscious of the gap between the freedom of his works and current taste, and kept most of these studies in his studio where they remained until his death.

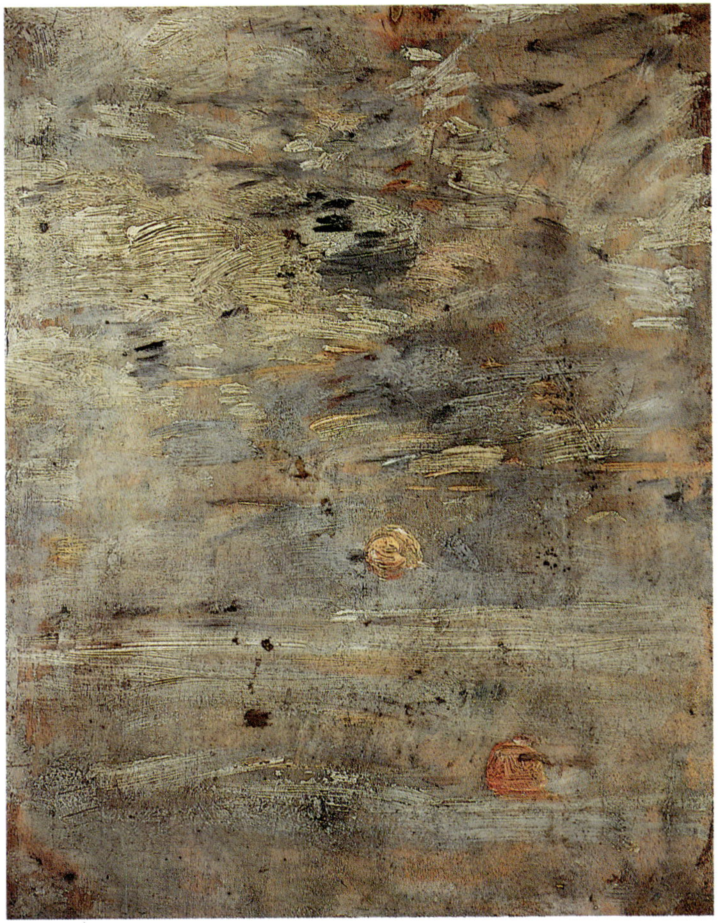
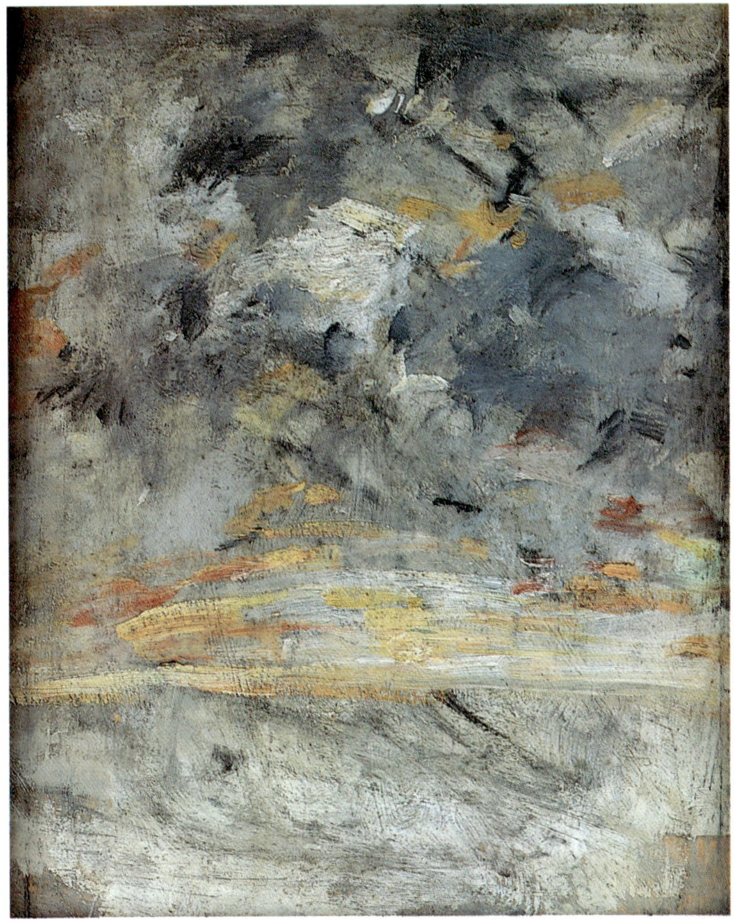

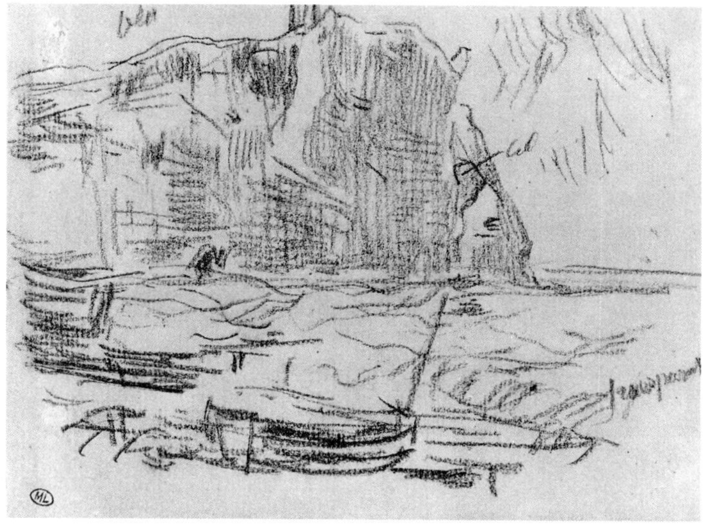

BOATS ON THE BEACH AT ÉTRETAT

1890-1894

Oil on panel, 38 x 58 cm, Beaux-Arts Museum, Le Havre

Above: pencil, Louvre Museum, Paris

In 1890 and 1891, Boudin made a couple of brief trips to Étretat. He was already familiar with the place since he had already been there before in 1854 when he had been doing more drawing than painting and was above all interested in the fishermen's lives. Here, however, the landscape is the real subject, even if the world of the fishermen is alluded to by the presence of boats, capstans, ropes and *calloges* (the boats covered in thatch, seen on the right-hand side of the painting). We can see perfectly how Boudin's drawing and painting techniques converge. The brushwork, like the line drawing, consists of parallel applications, to portray the strata of the cliff. But Boudin has attenuated the cliff's overpowering presence by tricks of light and by the importance given to the sky, thereby avoiding any impression of being hemmed in.

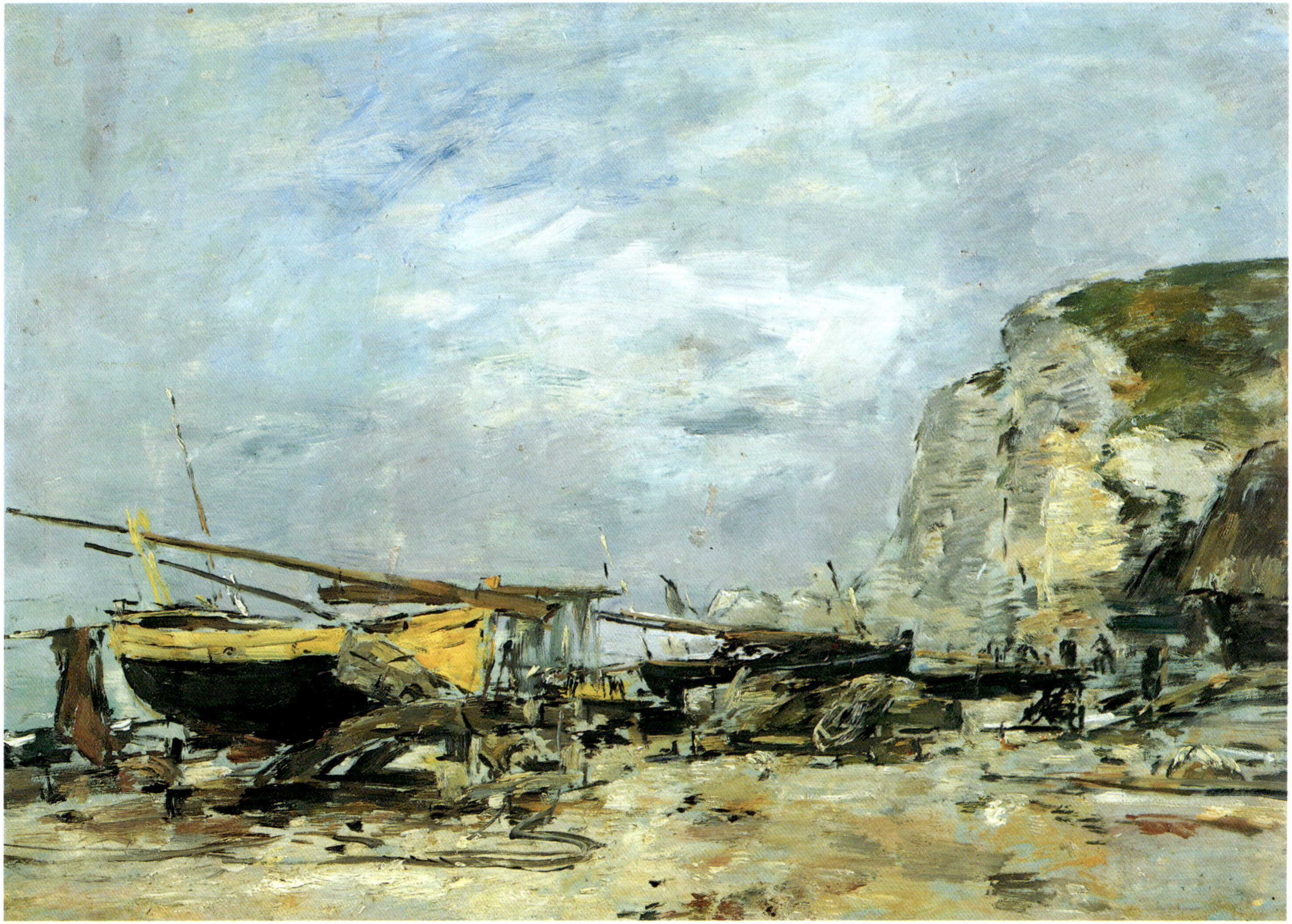

THE PORT OF ANTIBES

1893

Oil on canvas, 46 x 66 cm

Orsay Museum, Paris

At the beginning of spring 1893, Boudin went to Antibes. He was not used to the «bright skies» of the south of France, and hesitated to comment on his first attempts to portray it. Despite a difficult start, he eventually waxed enthusiastic for the region: «I started to work with an ardour worthy of a young man... I work eight hours a day like a common labourer but as it is in the open air and by the sea [...] I can keep up this rhythm, though it might kill a younger man.» He finally became conscious of the special quality of light in the south of France. His palette became lighter, his brushwork more transparent and his colours brighter. The painting shown here, donated to French museums by the Duchess of Windsor, is typical of this development. It is a most harmonious composition, in which horizontals dominate and where warm and cool tones are balanced to give an impression of serenity. The sky is treated with extraordinary delicacy and the fortifications seem to radiate light, as do the clouds in the background. Even the shadows appear bright. Boudin plays with the relationship between the ochre rocks in the foreground and the roofs of the town. The calm, peaceful sea is in the same lavender tones as the misty mountains in the background.

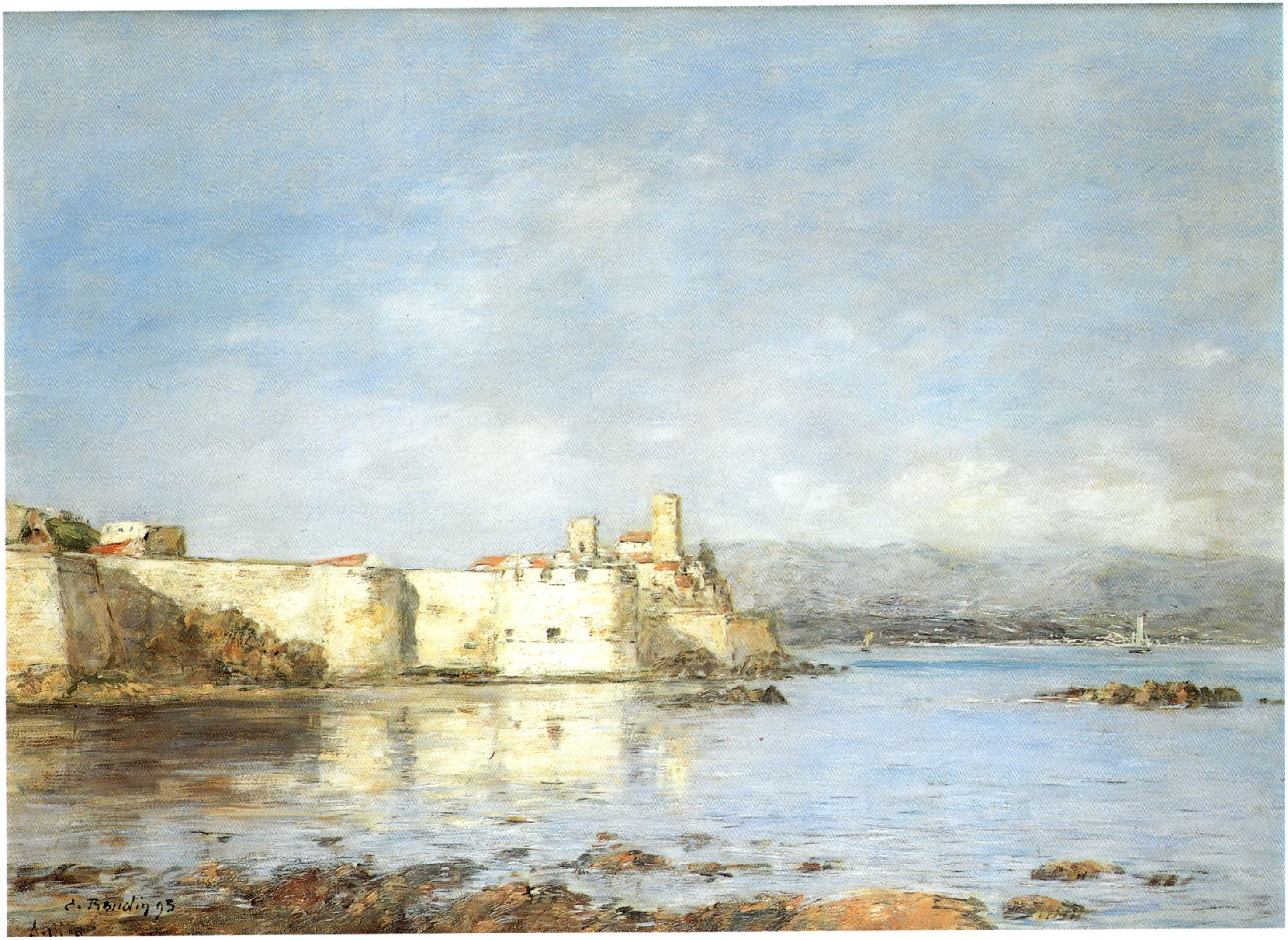

SUMMER IN TROUVILLE

c. 1894-1897

Oil on canvas, 40 x 74 cm

Beaux-Arts Museum, Le Havre

In 1884, with the financial backing of Durand-Ruel, Boudin decided to build a house in rue Oliffe in Deauville. «My wife says it looks like one of those Dutch cages in the shape of a house and that only the hook is missing to hang it up by.» In 1889, he moved in his «little country studio» and, from that time on, between travels and his winters in Paris, the "villa Marinette" which was renamed "villa Juliette", became his base, and it was there that he died in 1898. A mere stone's throw away from this «cabin with the red roof» were the views which were Boudin's special delight and which he painted several times, notably at times when «the Parisians have completely disappeared». But, as he himself said of *Plage de Trouville* (a beach in Trouville) done during the same period, painting such a vast, empty landscape is «a sort of tour de force and, since the painting has no hidden features, no shadows or contrasts, it is difficult to know how to give it the right warmth of lighting».

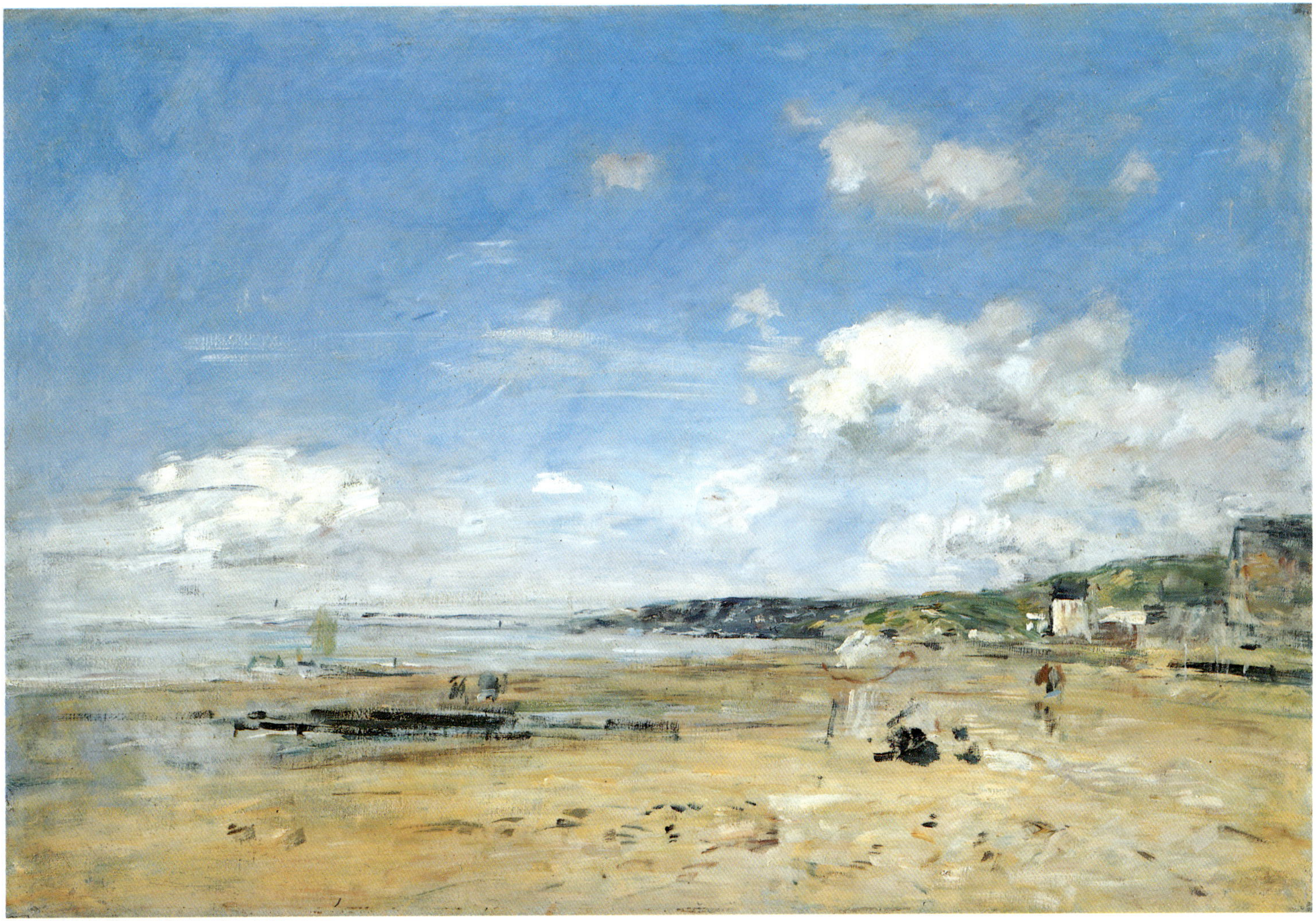

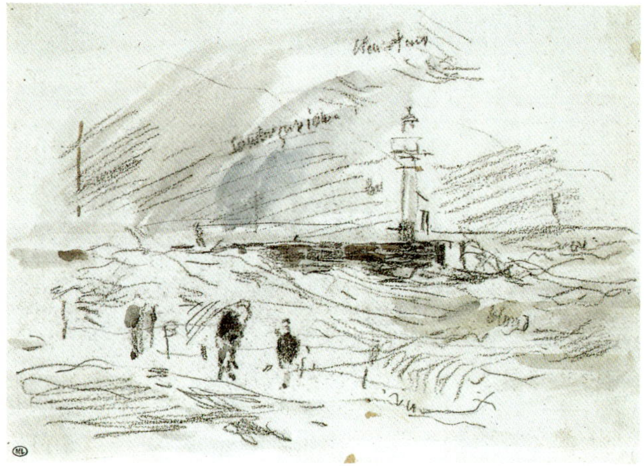

THE JETTIES OF LE HAVRE IN BAD WEATHER

1895

Oil on canvas, 51 x 75 cm, Beaux-Arts Museum, Le Havre

Above: pencil, watercolour, Louvre Museum, Paris

During the last years of his life when his health was failing, Boudin was obliged to abandon the practice of painting in the open air. He used a traditional method of working: drawing from life, sketching in oils «either on the spot or while the impression remained fresh», then completing the painting in the studio. The works seen here are preparatory studies for a final painting which is in a private collection. Another version, called *Coup de vent devant Frascati, Le Havre* (gust of wind in front of Frascati's, Le Havre), was exhibited at the 1897 Salon and bought by the City of Paris (now at the Petit-Palais Museum).

Although Boudin does not often show the elements unleashed, when he does so, he manages to render their power extremely well. In the oil sketch, greys dominate, giving the impression of an overcast sky, whilst in the final work, nearer to the watercolour sketch, greens dominate, thereby creating a cold harmony, reinforced by the white of the spray, the lighthouse and a cloud.

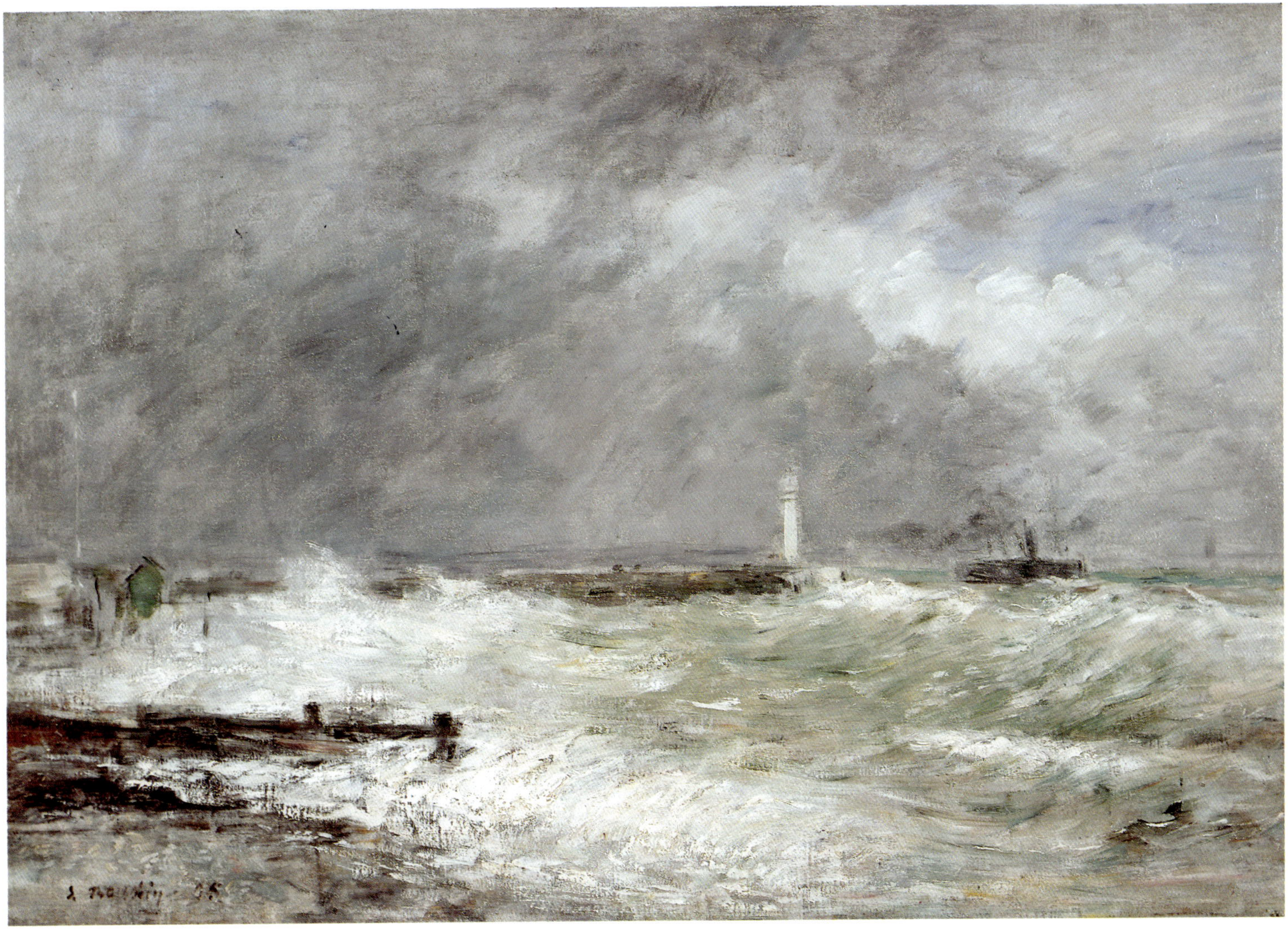

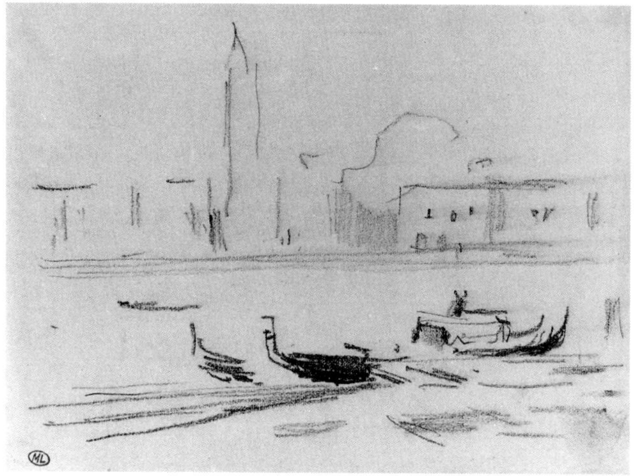

VENICE, THE HARBOUR AND THE SAN BIAGIO CHURCH

1895

Oil on panel, 20.6 x 39.5 cm, Beaux-Arts Museum, Rheims

Above: *View of San Giorgio*, c. 1892-1894, graphite, Louvre Museum, Paris

«For the moment, I am busy with some views of Venice – a superb city – I don't need to tell you that, but it has often been badly translated onto canvas by painters who have wrongly shown it in a hot, blistering sunlight. Like all other places full of light, Venice is grey, the air is soft and misty, and the sky is full of clouds just like those that grace the skies of Normandy or the Netherlands.» Boudin loved the delicate tones and the greys and, as always a complete master of his palette, took great pleasure in working in Venice where, as he suggested, the air was saturated with water, as in Normandy and the Netherlands, giving the colours a most subtle brilliance. It had doubtless been one of his secret desires to paint the "pearl of the Adriatic", but was also an obsessive fear. The following year, he came to the following conclusion: «The trip to Venice was my swan-song.»

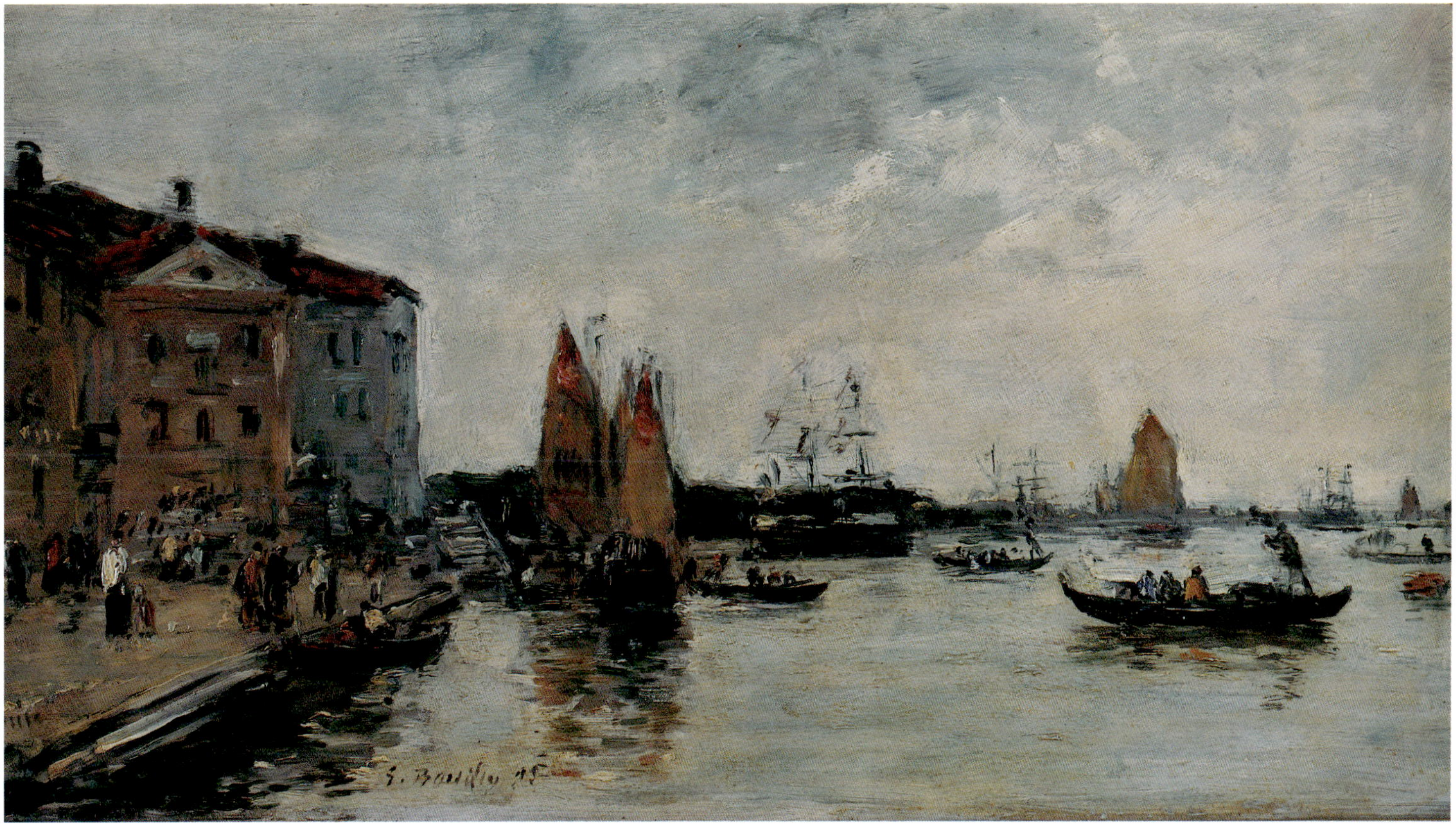

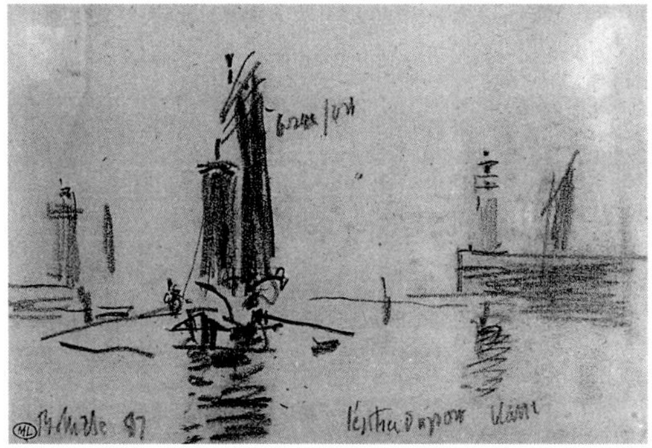

DOUARNENEZ, THE BAY SEEN FROM TRISTAN ISLAND

——— c. 1897 ———

Oil on canvas, 36 x 58 cm, private collection

Above: *Belle-Ile,* pencil, Louvre Museum, Paris

In the spring of 1897, Boudin took a last trip to Brittany. The visit lasted two months and took him from Le Pouliguen to Douarnenez. He wanted to see once again the places he had visited thirty years before, and to discover others that his fellow painters, notably Monet and Gauguin, had since discovered, such as Belle-Ile, la Pointe du Raz and Pont-Aven. During his first time to Brittany in 1855, Boudin had drawn the port of Douarnenez with a particular emphasis on the life of the fishermen, as in Honfleur (p. 13). His rather staid descriptive style of that period gave no foretaste of what would characterise his works of forty years later: a blaze of pictorial splendour and evocative line, combined with remarkable restraint. In this ambitious work, Boudin transposes the result of his studies of sky and sea (p. 51). The bringing together of sky, sea and earth at nightfall is merely an excuse for a brilliant and powerful study in colour, combined with visibly separate brushstrokes, made necessary by the forms of the clouds, the waves and the rocks. It is obvious that in this type of work, the subject (in this case a sunset) retains its meaning, and this is a fundamental difference with non-figurative painting. However, the place which inspired the work is of minimal importance.

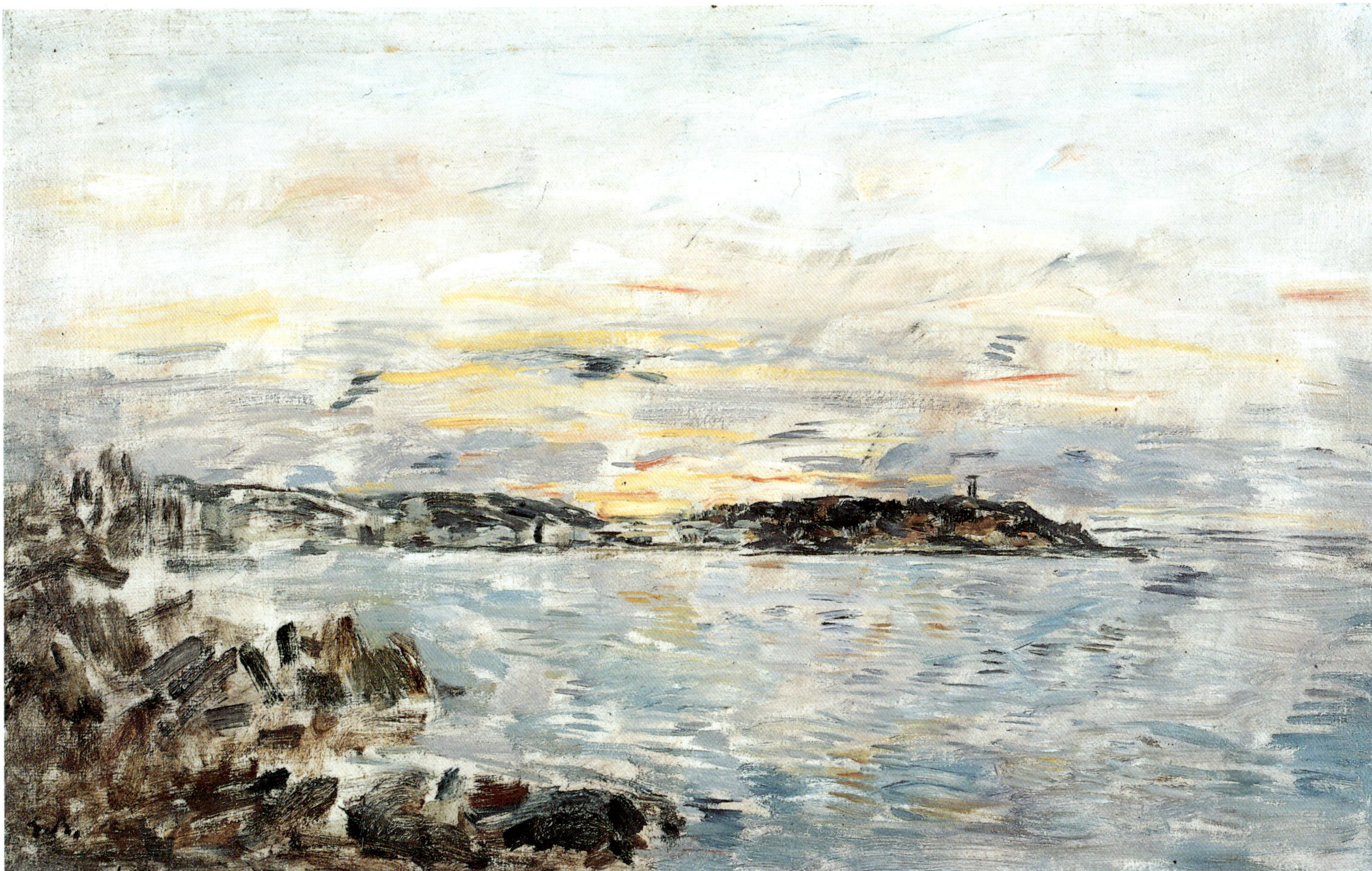

Biographical details

1824 : born in Honfleur.
1835 : the Boudin family moves to Le Havre.
1836 : starts work for a printer.
1844 : sets up a stationer's in partnership.
1846 : devotes himself to painting.
1851 : receives a grant from Le Havre to study for 3 years in Paris.
1854 : returns to Le Havre, stays in Honfleur for a while.
1855 : first visit to Brittany.
1858 : meets Monet in Le Havre.
1859 : meets Courbet in Le Havre and Baudelaire in Honfleur. Paintings hung for first time at Paris Salon.
1862 : meets Jongkind in Honfleur.
1863 : marriage in Le Havre. Starts a pattern which will rarely vary: winter in Paris, summer on the coast.
1870 : leaves for Belgium.
1872 : assures Courbet, who is in prison, of his faithful friendship.
1874 : beginning of the crisis in the art market.
1881 : Durand-Ruel buys his complete stock.
1888 : the State buys for 1.200 F *Une corvette russe dans le bassin de l'Eure – Le Havre* (Russian corvette in the Eure basin, Le Havre) for the Luxembourg Museum in Paris.
1889 : death of his wife. Puvis de Chavannes visits him in Deauville.
1890 : exhibits from now on with the Société Nationale des Beaux-Arts (National Fine Arts Society).
1891 : saddened by the death of his friends Jongkind and Ribot.
1892 : made chevalier de la Légion d'Honneur (civil decoration).
1897 : failing health.
1898 : dies in Deauville, and is buried in the Saint-Vincent cemetery in Montmartre.

Selected bibliography

Gilbert De Knyff: *Eugène Boudin raconté par lui-même. Sa vie – son atelier – son œuvre*, Mayer et De Knyff, Paris, 1976.

Denise Delouche: *Eugène Boudin et la Bretagne*, URSA, 1987.

Gérard Jean-Aubry: *Eugène Boudin. La vie et l'œuvre d'après les lettres et les documents inédits*, Paris, 1922. Reprints : Ides et Calendes, Neuchâtel, 1977 ; with the collaboration of Robert Schmit, Paris, 1988.

Pascale Lemoine: *Boudin roi des ciels*, Bibliothèque des Arts, Lausanne, 1981.

Laurent Manœuvre: *Eugène Boudin dessins*, Anthèse, Paris, 1991.

Laurent Manœuvre: *Boudin et la Normandie*, Herscher, Paris, 1991.

Robert Schmit: *Eugène Boudin, catalogue raisonné de l'œuvre peint,* Paris, 1973, suppl., Paris, 1984, et Paris, 1993.

Jean Selz: *Eugène Boudin*, Paris, 1983.

Exposition Boudin, catalogue, Honfleur, 1992.

The author

Laurent Manœuvre is an art historian in charge of the official databases of French museums. He has already published several works on Boudin as well as *Manet - Paris* by Éditions Herscher.

Credits

Our grateful thanks to the curators of the Eugène Boudin museum in Honfleur and the Beaux-Arts museum in Le Havre. We also thank Manuel and Robert Schmit and all the private collectors who have preferred to remain anonymous, for their help in preparing this work.

Cover: *The Trouville jetty,* 1869, oil on canvas, 64.8 x 92.8 cm, The Burrell Collection, Glasgow Museums.
Half-title page: *Le Havre regatta,* 1892-1896, oil on panel, 27 x 21 cm, Beaux-Arts Museum, Le Havre.
Frontispiece: *Trouville coastline,* 1894-1897, oil on canvas, 52 x 81.5 cm, private collection.
Page 5: *Fishermen off Le Havre,* 1852, oil on panel, 20 x 26 cm, Magnin Museum, Dijon.
Page 6: *Seine estuary near Honfleur,* 1854-1860, pastel on blue paper, 15.6 x 19.7 cm, private collection.
Page 7: *On the beach at Trouville,* 1863, oil on panel, 18.3 x 27.3 cm, private collection.
Page 8: Left: *Clouds, blue sky and boats,* 1895-1897, oil on panel, 23 x 32 cm, Beaux-Arts Museum, Le Havre.
Right: *Dusk over the Bassin du Commerce,* 1892-1894, oil on canvas, 40 x 55 cm, Beaux-Arts Museum, Le Havre.
Page 9: Left: *On the beach,* 1888-1895, oil on panel, 13 x 18 cm, Beaux-Arts Museum, Le Havre.
Right: *Cows by a river,* 1881-1888, oil on canvas, 32 x 46 cm, Beaux-Arts Museum, Le Havre.
Page 10: *Sky and white clouds over the estuary,* 1854-1860, pastel on beige papier, 15 x 20 cm, Boudin Museum, Honfleur.
Page 11: *Sailing boats,* 1885-1890, oil on panel, 24.5 x 33.5 cm, Orsay Museum, Paris.

Photo credits:
All the sources are credited on the appropriate pages, with the exception of: Pages 5, 11, 25, 33, 55 © R.M.N. Pages 16, 18, 26, 28, 31, 52, 58, 60 musée du Louvre/Département des arts graphiques des musées du Louvre et d'Orsay, Paris ; Back cover : Archives Durand-Ruel.

Layout: D.A. Graphisme/Daniel Arnault

ISBN : 2-7335-0277-8

Imprimé en France par I.M.E. - 25110 Baume-les-Dames
Dépôt légal : Septembre 2001
N° d'édition : 080277-02 - N° impression : 15419